RAPTURE, BLISTER, BURN

BY **GINA GIONFRIDDO**

★

★

DRAMATISTS
PLAY SERVICE
INC.

RAPTURE, BLISTER, BURN
Copyright © 2013, Gina Gionfriddo

All Rights Reserved

SPECIAL NOTE

SPECIAL NOTE ON SONGS AND RECORDINGS

For my mother.

RAPTURE, BLISTER, BURN was produced at Playwrights Horizons (Tim Sanford, Artistic Director; Leslie Marcus, Managing Director; Carol Fishman, General Manager) in New York City, opening on June 12, 2012. It was directed by Peter DuBois; the set design was by Alexander Dodge; the costume design was by Mimi O'Donnell; the lighting design was by Jeff Croiter; the sound design was by M.L. Dogg; the production manager was Christopher Boll; and the production stage manager was Lisa Ann Chernoff. The cast was as follows:

CATHERINE .... Amy Brenneman
ALICE .... Beth Dixon
AVERY .... Virginia Kull
GWEN .... Kellie Overbey
DON .... Lee Tergesen

RAPTURE, BLISTER, BURN was produced at the Geffen Playhouse in Los Angeles, California, opening on August 13, 2013. It was directed by Peter DuBois; the set design was by Alexander Dodge; the costume design was by Mimi O'Donnell; the lighting design was by Jeff Croiter and Jake DeGroot; the sound design was by M.L. Dogg; the production manager was Christopher Boll; and the production stage manager was Lisa Ann Chernoff. The cast was as follows:

CATHERINE .... Amy Brenneman
ALICE .... Beth Dixon
AVERY .... Virginia Kull
GWEN .... Kellie Overbey
DON .... Lee Tergesen

CHARACTERS
(in order of appearance)

CATHERINE CROLL, early 40s

ALICE CROLL, 70s

AVERY WILLARD, 21

GWEN HARPER, early 40s

DON HARPER, early 40s

TIME and PLACE

A college town in New England, summer.

RAPTURE, BLISTER, BURN

ACT ONE

Scene 1

Don and Gwen Harper's backyard in a New England college town. Night. June. A long table with citronella candles and two hardback books written by Catherine, who has just arrived moments ago. Catherine and Don sip beers; Gwen sips a bottle of water. It's the awkward lull after the big hellos. What now?

GWEN. I knew this wouldn't be weird. And you know what? I knew it that night you called.
CATHERINE. Really?
GWEN. Yes. That we were able to just chat like that after ten years ... That's true friendship — when a whole decade doesn't matter.
CATHERINE. It's more than a decade actually.
GWEN. Is it? Let's see. Julian was a baby when we went to New York for Christmas. He's thirteen, so ... You're right.
DON. That was a terrible day.
CATHERINE. Oh, good! Can we say that now?
DON. It was a terrible day and it was all her idea.
GWEN. It was my idea. You're crazy with the first kid. You think everybody has to meet the baby and ... not everybody does. Daddy's ex-girlfriend maybe didn't have to meet the baby.
CATHERINE. And maybe not at Christmas ...
GWEN. I was an idiot. But look at us! We're joking around like we're back in grad school. And it isn't weird!

DON. It's weird, Gwen. Just embrace it.

GWEN. *(After a beat.)* OK, Don told me not to say this, it'll make things weird ...

DON. Don't say it.

GWEN. I need to say that we're proud of you.

CATHERINE. Thank you.

GWEN. I quit drinking.

CATHERINE. You mentioned that.

GWEN. I had a problem. And part of my recovery is about, you know, expressing feelings, not drinking them down. So I need to say that I feel very proud of your achievements.

CATHERINE. Gwen, that means a lot to me. *(The doorbell rings — off.)*

GWEN. Babysitter! I'm gonna go get them settled. *(Gesturing.)* Oh! Don, make sure she signs our books.

DON. Yeah. *(Gwen runs inside to get the door. More silence. Then ...)* She sorta gave up drinking and took up talking.

CATHERINE. I can see that.

DON. But she really means it. And I do, too.

CATHERINE. Do you?

DON. Are you kidding? When you were on TV that time, we made Julian watch.

CATHERINE. Which time was that?

DON. It was the, uh, the late night show. On cable. You know ... where the comedian talks current events with a panel of mismatched experts —

CATHERINE. Bill Maher.

DON. Yeah, that one. When they introduced the panel, Julian was like, your friend is a senator? We said no. Then he's like, your friend is a rapper? I said no, she's the hot chick sitting between the senator and the rapper.

CATHERINE. Yep, that's me. My credibility falls somewhere between senator and rapper.

DON. What'd he call you ... the "hot doomsday chick"?

CATHERINE. Yeah ...

DON. That's ... You got the sexy scholar gig. We were proud as hell of you.

CATHERINE. That makes me really happy, Don. Thanks. *(Don opens his arms — a cautious invitation to a hug. They hug.)*

DON. I'm sorry about your mom. She doing OK?

8

CATHERINE. She's recovering. *(Gwen reenters.)*

GWEN. So we have a problem with our babysitter.

DON. What's that?

GWEN. She has a black eye.

DON. Oh, shit. What happened?

GWEN. Don't know, don't care. The problem is that she's upstairs with our three-year-old.

DON. Then we can go ...

GWEN. She has a black eye.

DON. You want me to find out what happened?

GWEN. I don't care what happened! Don, we can't just say bye-bye to Devon like this is normal, like someone punching out his babysitter is no big deal.

DON. Let me go see what's up ...

GWEN. Pay her and send her home.

DON. Then we can't go to dinner.

GWEN. Pay her and send her home. *(He leaves. Gwen joins Catherine. Her mood has changed.)* Did Don have you sign our books?

CATHERINE. No.

GWEN. Of course he didn't. Would you?

CATHERINE. Sure. To Don and Gwen?

GWEN. Yeah. Thanks. *(A beat, as Catherine signs.)* There's backstory here. Generally I care about people's injuries.

CATHERINE. What's the backstory?

GWEN. Let's see. Twelve years of backstory. Where to begin? Don doesn't teach anymore.

CATHERINE. You mentioned that.

GWEN. He's some sort of disciplinary dean. Isn't that crazy? He deals with kids who are drinking and failing, which ... I mean, it's Don. What does he know better than drinking and failing? So all these irresponsible children come through his office and what he does is he hires the most intriguing cases to "help" me. So I have a babysitter with a black eye and my lawn is ... Don hired some dopehead to mow it and he never shows.

CATHERINE. Nice he tries to help them.

GWEN. That's not why he does it. He just likes to surround himself with losers. *(Catherine hands Gwen the signed books. Gwen looks at them.)* Thanks. I guess the grass is always greener. It's just ... It's what you said, right? It's that forty-something thing where you start thinking about the life not lived.

CATHERINE. When did I say that?

GWEN. The night you called. You don't remember?

CATHERINE. I was sort of … drunk.

GWEN. I know. We used to drink so much. The three of us.

CATHERINE. We were young.

GWEN. Don never really stopped. I guess you didn't either.

CATHERINE. I drink pretty modestly. Since my mom's heart attack, I've been hitting it kinda hard. What else did I say that night?

GWEN. You were hilarious. You just spat out all these needs, like … "I'm drunk and my mom is dying and I'm coming home and I need a job." She's not really dying, is she?

CATHERINE. She had a heart attack. Both her sisters had heart attacks and died within the year, so … I feel like a clock just started ticking.

GWEN. Oh, no.

CATHERINE. Thank you for … I know you got Don to give me this teaching gig.

GWEN. Oh, please. He should get a promotion out of this. You're Miss New York Ivy League famous …

CATHERINE. Well, it came together so fast; I just know you must have helped it along.

GWEN. Because Don's so lazy and slow? Yeah, I nudged, but that's what I do for him. I'm keeper of his to-do list.

CATHERINE. September's so far away. I wish I'd asked to teach summer school.

GWEN. Tell Don. And I'll put it on his list. If I put it on his list, it'll happen. *(They sit in silence for a beat.)*

CATHERINE. What else did I say that night? I'm not a blackout drunk. This is … special circumstances. My mom.

GWEN. I know. You said you didn't want to be angry at us anymore. You forgave us.

CATHERINE. That was generous of me. *(Don enters.)*

GWEN. Is she gone?

DON. They're watching *Bob the Builder.*

GWEN. Why is she still here?

DON. Gwendolyn, I'm gonna tell you something about our little guy. You may not want to hear it …

GWEN. I know what you're going to say.

DON. *(To Catherine.)* Julian, our older son? Very sensitive soul. Our little guy, Devon, he's just not that way.

10

GWEN. Stop.

DON. The fact you don't want to face is that Devon hasn't noticed the girl has a black eye.

GWEN. He hasn't said anything. That doesn't mean he hasn't noticed.

DON. He hasn't noticed. He's a narcissist.

GWEN. He's three!

DON. He's happy. And we have dinner reservations.

GWEN. What is going to become of him if we let him think his insensitivity is OK?

DON. What will become of him? All kinds of good things. He can be a billionaire CEO; he can be president … *(Catherine and Don make eye contact, together in seeing humor in all this.)*

GWEN. It's not funny.

DON. We can't all be empathic. Nothing would ever get done.

GWEN. If we go to dinner, we are sending him a message that a girl with a black eye is no big deal.

DON. So you wanna throw her out, you wanna fire her —

GWEN. Yes.

DON. You wanna teach him battered women should be punished?

CATHERINE. He has a point.

GWEN. I said go ahead and pay her.

DON. I just don't like kicking her when she's down. Her boyfriend's a dick —

GWEN. It was her boyfriend?

DON. No, but it's his fault. He put her in harm's way.

CATHERINE. How'd he do that?

DON. Oh … He's a rich kid from California, thinks he's a filmmaker … They're over in Rocksboro filming people in line for lottery tickets. I'll deal with him next week. Let's go eat.

GWEN. Someone needs to tell Devon that a black eye is a bad thing.

DON. Not me. *(A beat. Is this a stand-off?)* He's got a lifetime to learn about human cruelty. Let him have his fucking magic years.

GWEN. OK, I'll talk to him. *(Gwen goes into the house.)*

DON. We could make a run for it. Skip dinner, go to a bar and get hammered …

CATHERINE. That sounds wonderful.

DON. I saw your mother at the Stop n' Shop. She looks pretty good for a lady who just had a heart attack.

CATHERINE. She shouldn't be out shopping. That's partly why I came home.

DON. If you need errands done, I got a teenager who'll do 'em for next to nothing.

CATHERINE. Your sensitive son?

DON. Julian, yeah. He's thirteen going on thirty-five. You gotta meet him. He wants to be an actor.

CATHERINE. Really?

DON. Yeah … He sings, he dances. I'm hoping he changes his mind. We need these kids to bankroll our old age.

CATHERINE. Sounds like you got a good shot at it with Devon.

DON. Hope so. You want another beer?

CATHERINE. I'm OK. But speaking of alcohol … I am in the awkward position of not remembering everything I said when I called that night.

DON. We were surprised as hell to get that call … Were you at a bar or something?

CATHERINE. Outside a bar, yeah.

DON. Did you still have our number in your phone?

CATHERINE. Oh, no. I had to call information.

DON. You drunk-dialed information. Well, isn't that something?

CATHERINE. It's humiliating.

DON. It's fantastic. You can memorize ten digits drunk.

CATHERINE. No, you can just … stay on the line while they connect the call.

DON. Oh, yeah?

CATHERINE. It costs like a dollar-fifty. Don, please don't fuck with me. I asked Gwen and I can tell she's holding back.

DON. Honey, I don't know. I was downstairs on the computer.

CATHERINE. I have this feeling I said things that should embarrass me.

DON. If you did, I'd know about it; Gwen can't keep anything to herself. *(They look at each other. A beat.)*

CATHERINE. I know we're all set for the fall, but do you have anything this summer?

DON. What, like summer school?

CATHERINE. I need something to do. Besides hang out with my mom and drink.

DON. Summer's already registered, but … Let me see if anyone has a waiting list.

CATHERINE. Thanks.

DON. You drinking too much?

CATHERINE. A little.

DON. Sick mother gives you a pass.

CATHERINE. I don't want a pass. I want to teach summer school.

DON. OK. I'll see what I can do. *(Avery enters.)* Avery, my friend. What's the story? We going out or ordering in?

AVERY. I don't know what you're doing, but I'm going home.

DON. Well, let me pay you …

AVERY. She already did. *(To Catherine.)* But she said before I go I should meet you because you're famous and you write about what I do.

CATHERINE. Babysitting?

AVERY. Yeah, ha ha. The babysitting is a side thing. I'm making a reality show with this guy I'm seeing.

DON. That's how she got the eye.

AVERY. Gwen said if I read your books I'll break up with him and stop making the show.

CATHERINE. That seems like a lot to ask of my books.

AVERY. Are those your books?

CATHERINE. Yeah.

DON. *(Getting up.)* I'm gonna dig out the takeout menus. Sorry, Avery. She's the boss of me when it comes to kid rearing.

AVERY. It's OK. *(Don goes into the house. A beat or so while Avery looks at Catherine's books.)* What are your books about?

CATHERINE. Well … The first one is about the politics of pornography within the women's movement …

AVERY. This one?

CATHERINE. Yeah. It has a terrible, hard-to-explain title that I regret.

AVERY. *(Reading.)* *Women Always Call Free: Pornography and the Corruption of American Feminism.* You're right. That's a bad title.

CATHERINE. You're too young to get it. One of the reasons it's a lousy title.

AVERY. "Women always call free." What does that even mean?

CATHERINE. Well. Back in the dark ages before the Internet, you had telephone sex lines. Men would call in and pay thirty cents a minute to talk dirty with women who were called phone sex workers.

AVERY. Seriously?

CATHERINE. Seriously. Why does that surprise you?

AVERY. It's just hard to imagine guys got off on that, you know? A voice.

CATHERINE. It does seem prehistoric, post-Internet. Now you just point and click to see full penetration.

AVERY. I guess it's like ... There used to be silent movies. And people went to them.

CATHERINE. And before television, families gathered around a radio.

AVERY. So intense. So the title ... *Women Always Call Free*?

CATHERINE. Yes. The sex lines were profitable, but a chunk of the profits went to paying the women. So eventually they tried phone sex lines without paid women answering the phones.

AVERY. So who did the men talk to?

CATHERINE. The idea was for both men and women to call in simultaneously. Then a computer would put them on the phone together. And the ads for these new sex lines said, "Women always call free." Because they knew that women would not pay to talk dirty with men. Men would pay, women wouldn't. So they had to let them call free. You follow?

AVERY. I know girls who would pay. Not a lot, but they'd pay.

CATHERINE. Right! Your generation of women would. How old are you?

AVERY. I'm twenty-one.

CATHERINE. You're half my age. The women of your generation have ... Let's say you have reduced inhibitions.

AVERY. You mean we're sluts.

CATHERINE. "Slut" is not in my lexicon. I said you're disinhibited.

AVERY. You think that's a bad thing?

CATHERINE. I think it's a very mixed thing.

AVERY. So did it work? Did the women call free?

CATHERINE. In comparatively small numbers.

AVERY. Did you call?

CATHERINE. Did I call? Uh ...

AVERY. You totally did. I would have, too. I mean, what the fuck? If it's free. What's your other book about?

CATHERINE. That book ... Well, I was contracted to write about the prison abuses at Abu Ghraib. The idea that the form the abuses took was influenced by Internet pornography.

AVERY. You think it was?

CATHERINE. Oh, I know it was. So I was supposed to write

about Abu Ghraib and porn but … It turned into a book about — more generally — how certain kinds of sadistic media are going to destroy us.

AVERY. That's heavy.

CATHERINE. It's very heavy.

AVERY. So it's about Internet porn?

CATHERINE. It's about the rise of degradation as entertainment.

AVERY. *(Reading.) Cruel Appetites: Internet Pornography, September 11th, and the Rise of Degradation as Entertainment.* Wow.

CATHERINE. Reality TV kinda takes a beating in there. That's probably why Gwen wants you to read it.

AVERY. So you blame 9/11 for the rise of degradation as entertainment?

CATHERINE. I think 9/11 and the Internet was kind of a perfect storm.

AVERY. God, that is so heavy. Can I borrow these?

CATHERINE. They're Gwen's.

AVERY. Then I'm definitely taking them. *(Takes the books.)* Cool. *(Starts to leave, then turns back to Catherine.)* Nice to meet you. *(As Avery goes into the house, Don comes out.)*

DON. So she's up there forcing him to sit through *Charlotte's Web.*

CATHERINE. If she's gonna teach him about violence, may as well cover death, too. *(Don smiles. A beat. The moment feels slightly flirtatious.)*

DON. So I have a proposal that includes you and me and whiskey.

CATHERINE. I'm in.

Scene 2

The home of Catherine's mother, Alice. Two weeks later. Alice sits while Catherine straightens up the room, preps it for her class.

ALICE. Now tell me again so I understand. It's the class you're teaching in the fall, but you're starting it now …

CATHERINE. They're running it first as a summer seminar. Only two students, so I'm going to hold class here. Is that OK?

ALICE. Oh, I don't mind. Do you have just a moment to go over my little list?

CATHERINE. Uh-oh. The little list.

ALICE. Now, I know you like an unscented soap. I think that's Ivory in your bathroom and that does have some perfume.

CATHERINE. I'll do a shopping run later.

ALICE. If you just tell me what brand you buy, I'll go.

CATHERINE. Mama, you had a heart attack; you are not gonna run around chasing my favorite soap.

ALICE. Cathy, just tell me.

CATHERINE. No!

ALICE. Well, I'm going out whether you like it or not because I know my coffee isn't hot enough for you.

CATHERINE. *(Parsing.)* It's not hot enough …

ALICE. You don't make your own coffee in New York. You buy it at a cafe and they have those big machines that make the coffee piping hot. I can't get it that hot in my little machine.

CATHERINE. It's summer, Mama, it doesn't have to be piping hot.

ALICE. But I can tell you don't like it. Now I could buy a percolator. The coffee will be very hot, but that's because it boils a little. Not everyone likes that.

CATHERINE. I like you relaxing at home. That's what I like.

ALICE. And I like making you happy.

CATHERINE. At least wait until after class and let me drive you …

ALICE. I feel wonderful! I wish I hadn't told you what happened. If I'd known you'd react this way —

16

CATHERINE. How did you think I'd react?

ALICE. I didn't think you'd leave your job and run home to me.

CATHERINE. It's a sabbatical; I didn't quit.

ALICE. You know, I was fine when my mother died. I was very briefly sad, then it was like a great burden had lifted. You know what they say: "Your life begins when your mother dies."

CATHERINE. Who says that? That's horrible.

ALICE. *(Trying to remember.)* Well, I heard it from my mother, but many people have said it.

CATHERINE. See! You were fine when your mother died because she said terrible things like that. *(Giving an order.)* You have to take care of yourself. I am not ready to live without you.

ALICE. You're over forty …

CATHERINE. Yes, but I didn't get married.

ALICE. So?

CATHERINE. So you are my beloved. You are the person who cares about what soap and coffee I like.

ALICE. A husband wouldn't care about those things.

CATHERINE. Great. Thank you. There goes my fantasy of filling the void left when you go.

ALICE. I'm not going anytime soon. *(After a beat.)* Why does Don take you out and leave his wife at home?

CATHERINE. I told you; they just fired their babysitter.

ALICE. Are you enjoying catching up?

CATHERINE. Yes. Very much. *(A beat. They look at each other and speak without speaking.)*

CATHERINE. He's married to Gwen.

ALICE. He was yours first and she took him from you.

CATHERINE. He was not "taken"; he went. I went to London, he married my roommate.

ALICE. Well, he asked you to come home and you said no …

CATHERINE. You agreed it was the right decision —

ALICE. You were young. I thought there would be other men. Better men.

CATHERINE. So what are you suggesting?

ALICE. You look so happy when you go out with him …

CATHERINE. Stop. They have children.

ALICE. I'm just suggesting you keep an open mind. I'm not planning on dying soon, but if you think a man would make that easier for you … Well, it's not too soon to think about getting one.

17

CATHERINE. Stop. I have to teach and if you start talking like that, I'll cry. Let's have our drinks at five like we always do. We can include the students. *(The doorbell rings.)*

ALICE. *(Rising.)* Oh, good. I'll be like your servant. I'll poke my head in at five and take everyone's drink order. First I'll get the door, though ... *(Alice leaves and answers the door. In a couple beats, Gwen and Avery enter.)*

CATHERINE. Gwen. And ... your ... babysitter.

AVERY. My name is Avery.

GWEN. Is this too weird?

CATHERINE. You're my two students?

GWEN. Don left your syllabus lying around and it completely blew me away. I'm gonna finish my degree. You've inspired me.

AVERY. I was signed up for another class, but I read your books and I think you're incredibly cool.

GWEN. *(Re: Avery.)* And we're OK! I mean, I fired her, but Don found her another job. It's not going to be a thing.

CATHERINE. Wow. I'm not gonna lie; this feels a little odd.

GWEN. It feels odd now, but it's gonna be great.

AVERY. Also, I mean ... We're the only ones who signed up. So you can be weirded out, but no us, no class.

CATHERINE. Did you both do the first day's reading? *(They indicate that they have.)* Then ... I guess ... Take your seats. *(They all take seats.)*

GWEN. *(To Avery.)* Catherine and Don and I went to graduate school together. We used to hit the bars after class ... Pitchers and pitchers of beer and ... fierce intellectual battles. Catherine was deconstructing and Don was all about the primacy of the text. So they would fight. Don had a beard and when he drank a lot he would become Walt Whitman. He would, like, preach his poems. It sounds annoying, but it was beautiful. People would gather to watch ...

CATHERINE. Don's Whitman looked a lot like Charles Manson.

GWEN. It did! Crazy eyes and all this hair.

CATHERINE. Never underestimate a hairy man who's memorized poetry.

GWEN. It was more than that. *(To Avery.)* Don used to be a very inspiring teacher. It was a very ... rich time in our lives. And I sometimes really miss it.

CATHERINE. So! *(Raising the syllabus.)* Welcome to "The Fall of American Civilization"! When I heard the class was only two people,

I thought … Why not be informal? We can have class here … drink wine or beer or whatever.

GWEN. Well, I don't drink, but —

AVERY. I drink.

GWEN. I'm FINE with other people drinking. So fine.

CATHERINE. Good. Well, it's a four o'clock class and five is when Mother and I have our drinks. So that gives us … enough time for me to hear why you took the course and what you hope to get from it. Gwen already said a little bit, so … Avery?

AVERY. Um … I'm Avery Willard. I signed up because … Well, you already know that.

CATHERINE. You're making a reality show with your boyfriend.

AVERY. He's actually not my boyfriend.

GWEN. They're "exclusively hooking up."

AVERY. No. We're hooking up exclusively.

GWEN. Isn't that what I said?

AVERY. No. Exclusively hooking up sounds like all we do is hook up. Which it isn't. We're starting a company together.

GWEN. Tell her about the show.

AVERY. The show is called *Town and Gown,* and it's Lucas and me interacting with townies.

GWEN. It's you getting drunk and Lucas filming it …

AVERY. *(Putting a hand up to silence her.)* The conceit of the show is that Lucas is behind the camera and I'm this agent provocateur who infiltrates various townie hang outs.

GWEN. Skip ahead to the part where you're stripping.

AVERY. Jesus, you're obsessed! One night, we met a stripper and she was cool so I went to work with her for a couple weeks. We got an episode out of it and it was really good for me emotionally.

GWEN. Stripping was good for you emotionally?

AVERY. I made ten times what you paid me to babysit. And it was good for my body image and my relationship with my parents. I'm not their bitch anymore.

CATHERINE. Avery, how exactly did you get punched?

AVERY. The lottery line in Rocksboro. See, I ask the provocative questions because Lucas says blue collar guys don't hit girls.

GWEN. Guess Lucas was wrong.

AVERY. Guess he wasn't. A girl hit me.

GWEN. This prince she's "hooking up exclusively" with? He filmed it all.

AVERY. That's what filmmakers do, Gwen, they film things. And right now he is interning in L.A. so that we can sell our show and have an awesome future.

GWEN. And what if he does sell it? Do you want the world to see you stripping and getting beat up?

AVERY. Gwen, you're gonna feel really stupid when this works out for me.

CATHERINE. OK. Well. We'll get into reality television towards the end of the course. We'll get into raunch feminism before that, which I think will also be relevant to you —

AVERY. What is raunch feminism?

CATHERINE. It's the belief that women can empower themselves by embracing sexual behaviors that carried a stigma for earlier generations. Things like stripping, sex without commitment …

AVERY. I definitely agree that stuff's empowering, but I don't personally identify as a feminist.

CATHERINE. Exactly. Let's get to work. *(Handing out syllabus.)* The course covers six units in three modules … Let's do this. Avery, you take the first module: "Gender Roles and Relationships." We're discussing that today. Are you ready to jump in?

AVERY. Sure. Why not?

CATHERINE. Then next week … Yikes. Next week is the "Cruel Appetites" module. That's torture horror and sadistic porn. I'll take that. Which leaves … Gwen, why don't you take module three … "The Death of Privacy." That's reality television and social networking. That sound OK to everyone? *(They nod "yes.")* OK! Let's start. Avery.

AVERY. You want me to, like, summarize the reading?

CATHERINE. Yeah. Summarize, inserting your point of view.

AVERY. OK. So … Feminism started in the Sixties …

CATHERINE. Well, the period relevant to this course begins in the Sixties, but —

AVERY. Right, I know. There was a "first wave" of feminism before that, but it's not interesting.

CATHERINE. It isn't?

AVERY. I mean, I'm glad it happened. It put an end to women being owned like slaves, and we got the right to vote. It's just … None of it is controversial, so what is there to talk about?

CATHERINE. It was controversial at the time, of course.

AVERY. I know, but … It's like discussing why people thought the

Earth was flat. It's not, they were wrong, we've moved on.

CATHERINE. Fair enough.

AVERY. So ... Second wave is in the 1960s and it's about ... It's about this "feminine mystique" idea that Betty Friedan wrote about.

CATHERINE. Great. What is the feminine mystique?

AVERY. She said basically women have been sold a bill of goods that being a housewife and a mom is fulfilling when it so totally isn't.

GWEN. That is not what Betty Friedan said.

CATHERINE. Yeah ... Avery, you want to take another stab at that?

AVERY. Why?

CATHERINE. Well, because Friedan's ideas are more nuanced than that. And the only other student in the class is a stay-at-home mom.

AVERY. Well ... What I got is that it's a recipe for misery for women to find all their happiness in husbands and kids. Because a husband can divorce you and kids grow up. If all you do with your life is serve people who leave you ... Well, then, you're fucked.

GWEN. Can I speak?

CATHERINE. Avery, motherhood is not the only job that a woman can age out of. I mean, arguably, a mother is a mother forever and a female tennis pro has her job for only a very few years.

AVERY. Yeah, but then she can coach or go on TV or sell sports drinks. She can make a ton of money. Where do you go after being a housewife?

GWEN. You're completely missing Friedan's point. The notion that a woman can only find fulfillment as a wife and mother? That happens to be true for me. But it's not true for Catherine. Do you see? What was revolutionary about Friedan was her assertion that all women do not fit one mold.

AVERY. Right. But I'm sorry ... Part of her argument is about how boring being a housewife is if you have a functioning brain.

CATHERINE. That's in there, but I think the salient point is choice.

AVERY. You aren't married and you don't have children.

CATHERINE. That's true, but not because I think being a wife and a mother is beneath me.

AVERY. OK, but ... Can I just be totally frank here?

CATHERINE. OK ...

AVERY. I read your Wikipedia entry. You cannot tell me that your achievements are not a way better destiny than, like, potty training and cutting crusts off bread.

CATHERINE. I can tell you that I'm not sure.

AVERY. Are you just saying that because she's in the room?

CATHERINE. No. It's the truth. My mother is going to die soon and I find myself wondering if there isn't some … wisdom in the natural order. In creating a new family to replace the one you lose.

AVERY. You can still have a family. I mean, if that's a big regret for you. *(To Gwen.)* And you can go back to work, I guess.

GWEN. I'm not complaining. I'm not unfulfilled.

AVERY. You will be, though. When Julian goes away to college, you're gonna have a humongous breakdown if you don't start planning now.

CATHERINE. OK, Avery.

GWEN. No, there's some truth to that. Julian's my best buddy. We go to New York once a month and see a show, and that's when I'm happiest. I don't know what my future looks like when he leaves home.

AVERY. Want me to tell you? Julian's gonna move to New York and get a posse of gay friends who don't want his mom hanging around. That is what's going to happen.

GWEN. I know. It's gonna be really hard.

AVERY. So, is the message that women are fucked either way? You either have a career and wind up lonely and sad, or you have a family and wind up lonely and sad?

CATHERINE. Maybe you have both and you wind up fulfilled.

GWEN. I don't know anyone who has that.

AVERY. I don't know if I want kids or not. I mean, I've thought about being a stay-at-home mom just as like a fuck-you to the system …

CATHERINE. How is being a stay-at-home mom a fuck-you to the system?

AVERY. Well, for starters, it would kill my parents. I've had like a million dollars' worth of education. If I wind up in Mommy and Me class after all that, their fucking heads will explode.

GWEN. Do not have a child to rebel against your parents.

AVERY. I know what I'm doing. I'm gonna do the career thing first, then if I decide I want kids later, I can hire someone to take care of them. If you choose the right career and the right husband, you can afford to outsource the homemaker shit.

GWEN. You think you can outsource homemaking?

AVERY. Yeah, I do.

CATHERINE. I don't think you can. I think I'm supposed to be impartial because I'm the teacher, but I don't think you can.

AVERY. If you have enough money, you can.

CATHERINE. I think you can hire someone to clean your house and cook your food and babysit your kids, but I don't think you can pay someone to create a home for you.

AVERY. Sure you can. It's called a decorator.

CATHERINE. Let me phrase this differently. I think a woman — a person — has a finite amount of energy and creativity, and if that all goes into your work ... *(A beat; to reveal or not to reveal.)* I hired a decorator and a cleaning woman and my apartment just looks like a fancy hotel now. It's cold. You can't outsource nesting.

AVERY. I think you can. It sounds like you just weren't communicating with your decorator. The point is you can hire people to do your home, but you can't hire people to do your career.

CATHERINE. OK. Let's just ... Let's agree that Betty Friedan was not about rejecting domesticity, she was about giving women a choice.

AVERY. OK, fine. Second wave feminism was about giving women equality with men ... equal opportunities, equal wages. But it was also about sex. There were hippies and they taught women it was OK to look at their vaginas. And we got the birth control pill and legalized abortion ...

CATHERINE. Great. So you recognize that these are all major gains.

AVERY. Oh, yeah. So ... Until like 1980, all the feminists were on the same page. Then some of them started freaking out about pornography. And the women's movement splits over this.

CATHERINE. What did you think about that split?

AVERY. I think you can't be a feminist and be anti-porn.

GWEN. Really?

AVERY. Yeah. If you believe a woman should be free to choose her own destiny, you can't add a "but" to that, like "You can choose your destiny unless it's sucking dick on film."

GWEN. Oh, my God ...

AVERY. What?

GWEN. You're in a classroom.

AVERY. What's wild is that the porn these women were freaking out over was … It was like the fucking *Care Bears* compared to what's on the Internet. And it was not that easy to get. Reading this stuff really helped me understand your generation.

CATHERINE. Well … We're not seventy. There was porn and you could get it. But there was a social shame around it and you had to go through gatekeepers to get it which carried risk.

AVERY. Like what kind of risk?

GWEN. To go to a video store for porn … You risked running into your boss, your child's teacher …

AVERY. You mean people looked down on you if you watched porn?

GWEN. Of course they did! And they should. That's gone now. Now porn is no big deal.

AVERY. It is if you watch too much of it and never get laid for real. Then people think you're a loser.

GWEN. Right. A guy of your generation who never gets laid would be a freak because girls today are … You're easy.

AVERY. But why is "easy" a bad thing, Gwen? What is the point of making sex difficult?

GWEN. Things that are easy have no value.

CATHERINE. Avery, you haven't discussed Phyllis Schlafly. She has some thoughts on "easy" women.

AVERY. I had to stop reading her, she pissed me off.

CATHERINE. She offends a lot of people. She is a woman in opposition to the women's movement.

AVERY. So why would you teach her?

CATHERINE. Because you should hear both sides of the major issues. And I think she has some valid points.

GWEN. I do, too.

CATHERINE. *(To Avery.)* Where did you stop reading?

AVERY. *(Searching …)* I highlighted the worst part … She was talking about the sad fate of the single, career woman. OK, here … *(Finding it.)* Schlafly thought the destiny of the liberated woman was: "a cold, lonely apartment whose silence is broken only by the occasional visits of men who size her up as … an easy mark for sexual favors for which they will never have to pay nor assume responsibility."

GWEN. Which part of that do you object to?

AVERY. Umm … All of it? Why does she call it a "sexual favor"? She makes it sound like women don't like sex, too. *(Alice peeks in …)*

ALICE. Is it too early for the martinis?

CATHERINE. Not at all.

GWEN. I don't drink anymore, but I can make drinks.

ALICE. I've already made them! And I made a Shirley Temple for Gwen!

GWEN. Oh, you're so sweet!

CATHERINE. Mama, drink yours in here with us because we might need you.

ALICE. Need me?

CATHERINE. I want a tri-generational perspective on this one. We're reading Phyllis Schlafly. *(Alice enters with small tray holding a martini shaker, a glass full of olives, and Gwen's Shirley Temple. Throughout the following, Catherine gets martini glasses from somewhere in the room and Alice pours and serves the drinks.)*

ALICE. Phyllis Schlafly … From the Seventies?

CATHERINE. Yes!

ALICE. Isn't she that beauty queen who advertised orange juice?

CATHERINE. No, but you're very close. Anita Bryant advertised orange juice and opposed equality for gay people. Phyllis Schlafly opposed equality for women.

GWEN. *(Re: Alice.)* You experienced the women's movement! We want your perspective.

ALICE. You know, I wasn't really aware. I know that's terrible. I was just very wrapped up in my little baby …

GWEN. It would have started before Cathy was born, though.

CATHERINE. What about the Equal Rights Amendment? Were you for or against?

ALICE. I suppose I was for it.

CATHERINE. You suppose? You don't remember?

ALICE. I married late; I'd waited so long to have my baby, you know … I only had eyes for her.

CATHERINE. So you don't remember Phyllis Schlafly opposing the ERA?

ALICE. No. Why did she do that?

CATHERINE. She believed that an Equal Rights Amendment would be the end of marriage. And the end of marriage would be the end of civilization.

ALICE. Why would the ERA end marriage?

CATHERINE. Her argument was that marriage and family are not natural states for men, so society has to force them into it. And the way to force them, she believed, was to shame them, tell them that women are the weaker sex and can't survive without them.

AVERY. But why? If the women all have jobs, too, they can take care of themselves.

CATHERINE. In their "cold, lonely apartments"?

AVERY. Is she saying if you have a career, men won't want to marry you?

CATHERINE. To be fair, these ideas don't originate with her; Rousseau said the same thing in the 1700s. He said men won't marry for love, but they will marry for vanity. A woman who shrinks and swoons makes a man feel good, feel strong.

AVERY. But it's all the same lie. Swooning, shaming ... It's the same lie that we're weaker —

ALICE. But I don't hear either of them saying that women are weaker. Are they saying that?

CATHERINE. No.

ALICE. So all they ask is that we create the appearance of weakness to inspire the men to take care.

CATHERINE. Correct.

ALICE. Well, I think they're right, and I don't think it's so terrible.

AVERY. So relationships are just an exercise in manipulation and deceit?

ALICE. Those are harsh words. Let's say they're an exercise in illusions.

AVERY. I think it's fucked up and demeaning.

CATHERINE. It's an idea we must seriously entertain, if for no other reason than it persists over centuries. Just last year my mother bought me a new book advocating the old swoon and shame. It's called *Love Smart* and it's by the contemporary philosopher Dr. Phil.

ALICE. If I'd sent you Rousseau, would I have been met with less ridicule?

CATHERINE. Yes, and I realize that isn't fair. They're saying the exact same thing.

ALICE. *(To Catherine.)* I really can't believe I'm hearing this. You made me feel so stupid for giving you that book ...

CATHERINE. Maybe I'm trying to learn from my mistakes.

AVERY. What mistakes did you make? I mean, it seems like you're kind of bummed out you're not married with kids.

ALICE. She is.

AVERY. Have you tried Internet dating?

CATHERINE. Let's leave my existential despair for another time.

GWEN. What do you mean, existential? It sounds like you just want a family.

CATHERINE. I say "existential" because it's … Well, here goes my professorial neutrality. Being alone wasn't a problem until I had to face losing my mother.

ALICE. You really have to stop this. I could live for years.

GWEN. Why didn't you get married? I mean … Shut me up if I'm out of line asking that.

CATHERINE. No, it's OK. This is why I wanted to teach Schlafly, you know. I detest her, but lately I think she has a point.

AVERY. What is the point?

CATHERINE. Look, Schlafly is very clear that when a man and woman come together, the man must lead and the woman must follow. Now, yes, that's an offensive notion when you put it out there as a rule. But my middle-aged observation is that … In a relationship between two people, you can't both go first.

ALICE. It's true, Cathy. *(Catherine puts up a finger to silence her.)*

CATHERINE. Stop. You always encouraged me to put myself first.

ALICE. And I still do! If I were you, I'd stay single. There'd be no existential anything.

GWEN. You think you're alone because you put your career first?

AVERY. Wait. Why does someone have to come first? What's wrong with 50/50?

CATHERINE. I think theoretically you can have 50/50. But on a practical, geographic level it's just very hard to do. It becomes a matter of, you know, is the other person willing to sacrifice and follow.

GWEN. And you were always leading, right? 'Cuz you're a superstar.

CATHERINE. When opportunities came, I took them.

AVERY. But why wouldn't your men follow you?

CATHERINE. Well, it puts us back to Schlafly. And Rousseau and Phil. Maybe men aren't hard-wired to follow women.

AVERY. My mother's second husband is. There are men who will follow you around. I'm just personally not attracted to them.

CATHERINE. *(Genuinely curious.)* Why is that, do you think?

AVERY. Umm … I want my guy to have a thing he's fired up about. Like politics or movies or saving the planet. I want him to have a thing; I do not want to be the thing. You get it?

CATHERINE. All right, let's say your man has a passionate interest that isn't you …

AVERY. That's ideal.

CATHERINE. Let's say it's … oceanography. And you get a fabulous job in a land-locked state. Let's say Kansas.

AVERY. It's not a fabulous job if it's in Kansas.

CATHERINE. Chicago, then. So you can't both have what you want. Let's say he is willing to put his oceanography on hold while you take this job …

AVERY. If he's willing to give it up that easily, then he didn't care enough about it.

CATHERINE. My point is that someone has to sacrifice. Feminism asserted — quite rightly — that women have a right to the same opportunities as men. What feminism has arguably left unfinished is how two empowered people are supposed to negotiate all this fantastic equality. Why must we think of male sacrifice as unmanly? It's not as though there aren't models for it. There's … Jesus.

ALICE. No worthwhile man wants to depend on a woman. I'm sorry; that is what I think.

CATHERINE. So when a woman follows a man, she's supportive; when a man follows a woman, he's a user?

ALICE. Cathy, it's how I was raised. It just doesn't seem natural to me.

GWEN. Let's not romanticize sacrifice too much. I mean, leave Jesus out of it; he was Jesus and he could rise again. For most of us, there's no rising again after you sacrifice.

AVERY. You feel like you sacrificed your career and now you're dead?

GWEN. No. I wasn't a passionate academic like Cathy and Don. It's not like I killed my soul by dropping out. *(To Avery.)* I dropped out of the program, you know. They finished, I didn't.

AVERY. So if your soul's OK, what's your problem?

GWEN. I didn't say I had a problem, Avery, I just don't think we should romanticize economic dependence. I can't teach with just an undergrad degree. I couldn't support my kids if I had to. Or if I … wanted to.

AVERY. Do you … want to?

GWEN. I don't think it's appropriate for me to say more.

AVERY. It's appropriate.

ALICE. Do you want another Shirley Temple?

GWEN. Umm … Sure.

CATHERINE. You don't have to bare your soul just because I did. We can move on.

AVERY. I was your babysitter, you know. I kinda know how your marriage works. *(A beat. Is Gwen going to vent? Sure would feel good. OK, why not?)*

GWEN. *(To Avery.)* I was a huge drunk when I hooked up with Don. Don was Catherine's boyfriend and I stole him.

AVERY. Nice.

GWEN. I know! Don is always disputing that I had an alcohol problem. But … Look what I did! *(To Catherine.)* You wish you'd had a family; I wish I'd finished school. We have no money. We live this lie in our nice house. You can be poor when your kids are little; they don't need much. It's when they get older … We're barely managing Julian's private school tuition; if we try to do it for Devon, it'll break us. And the public schools here are bad. The plan was for Don to work hard and get a better job — somewhere with decent schools. He didn't even try! See, I'm sober so this crisis is real to me in every moment. Don … He smokes pot, he drinks … He's tranquilized fifty percent of the time and it's kept him from bettering his life. Our life. There. I said it.

AVERY. What do you think he should have done?

GWEN. What Catherine did! *(To Catherine.)* I mean, you deserve everything you got, but Don is just as smart as you —

CATHERINE. He is.

GWEN. He could have written more books and gotten better jobs. Things really went downhill when he became a dean. It was a little more money for doing a lot less, and Don doesn't do well with free time.

AVERY. I got sent to Don because I partied too hard and got put on academic probation. He read me a William Blake poem about excess being the road to enlightenment.

GWEN. That's exactly it! He thinks a good life just … unfolds. He doesn't understand it takes work …

ALICE. And you do all the work.

GWEN. I don't mind doing all the work at home — home is my sphere. But work, money … that's supposed to be Don's sphere, and he has not held up his end. *(A beat.)* Also he has a porn issue.

ALICE. What kind of issue?

CATHERINE. Pornography.

ALICE. Oh!

AVERY. What kind of porn does he watch?

GWEN. I don't know.

CATHERINE. When you say issue ...

GWEN. He watches porn like other people watch *The Tonight Show*. It's like his private time after the kids go to bed.

AVERY. So you have no sex life?

CATHERINE. Avery —

GWEN. No. We don't.

CATHERINE. Can I ask a ... a perhaps too personal question?

GWEN. Sure.

CATHERINE. You have two children a decade apart.

GWEN. We had another baby instead of getting a divorce.

ALICE. Did that work?

GWEN. It helped. Now Don has someone who's crazy about him and Julian and I can have fun without feeling guilty.

AVERY. Devon is like the opposite of Julian.

GWEN. He chases the garbage truck. His favorite book is about a backhoe.

AVERY. Nice try naming him Devon, but ...

GWEN. He really is Don's kid. In a perverse way, having no money is the thing that keeps us together. If I was a trust fund baby, I'd go live in New York with the kids ... finish my degree, send the kids to Don on weekends. But we're poor. *(A beat and an exhale.)* Phew!! That felt good.

ALICE. *(After a beat.)* I thought about that ... having another child. Cathy and I just had so much fun together, and my husband didn't join in. I wondered if a fourth person would have helped.

CATHERINE. It wouldn't have.

ALICE. No. He provided well and he loved us. He just wasn't a family sort of person. If we had lived in a world that sanctioned a man being a lifelong bachelor, then that's what my husband would have been. But he couldn't be. Society frowned on unmarried men.

AVERY. What do you mean, they "frowned"?

ALICE. In my day, a man alone over thirty was suspect. It wasn't normal and people talked.

GWEN. They thought he was gay?

ALICE. Sometimes. More often, they just thought he was defective.

AVERY. What do you mean — "defective"?

ALICE. An odd bird. A lemon. Every man was expected to marry,

30

you see. So if you didn't, that meant no woman would have you. So you were considered defective and you couldn't succeed in your career the way a married man could.

AVERY. That's discrimination.

ALICE. *(To Avery.)* When I was your age ... You couldn't go out on Saturday night if you didn't have a date. Boys or girls. If you didn't have a date, you sat home with your mother. Period. I remember a party I wanted to go to ... All of my friends were going and I didn't have a date. So I couldn't go.

AVERY. What if you had just said ... Fuck that, I don't need a man and went by yourself?

ALICE. It just wasn't done.

AVERY. I know, but what if you just ... did it, what would have happened? *(Alice considers this. Then ...)*

ALICE. It would have turned the men off. I think it still turns them off, if you want my opinion.

CATHERINE. This is a favorite topic of my mother's. *(To Alice.)* What if you went to the party alone and you had sex with a man you met there?

ALICE. Big, big turn-off. No one buys the cow if he can get the milk for free.

AVERY. Wait. Giving the man sex would turn him off?

ALICE. These days, men aren't ashamed to be alone and women aren't ashamed to give them sex. So what incentive is left for the men to marry?

CATHERINE. Some of them have emotional needs, Mom. You can't generalize about all men based on Dad.

ALICE. All the incentives are gone!

AVERY. *(After a beat.)* You know what seems a little crazy? And sorry if this is rude, but ... We're having this big talk about how you force men to get married and it's like ... Rousseau says this and Schlafly says that. But from where I'm sitting ... both of your marriages sound horrible.

GWEN. You're right; that is rude. Say what you want to me, but Alice is a senior citizen.

ALICE. Oh, I don't mind ...

AVERY. *(To Gwen.)* Like you said, I'm in a classroom. I'm just pointing out a ... would this be a paradox or an irony?

CATHERINE. More of an irony, I think.

GWEN. You think your relationship offers a better model than —

31

AVERY. Than what I've heard today, yeah, I do. *(A beat. The women consider this.)* Well, I've learned a lot today. And not that I'm not enjoying the Ya-Ya Sisterhood we have happening, but I have to go to work.

GWEN. The class isn't over.

AVERY. Not enough notice to get a sub. Won't happen again.

GWEN. You're working for Professor Baron?

AVERY. That didn't pan out. I'm waitressing.

GWEN. Someplace decent?

AVERY. Not really. I'll see you Wednesday. *(Avery leaves. A beat.)*

GWEN. And that ... is what happens when a straight-A, pre-med student discovers beer and boys. Don says the late-bloomers fall the hardest. *(After a beat.)* So ... Next class! Sadism! I'm having such a good time and I knew I would. You're wonderful, Cathy, you really are. *(Gwen leaves. After a beat ...)*

ALICE. You can have him if you want him.

CATHERINE. Excuse me?

ALICE. Don. If you wanted to slip in, you could.

CATHERINE. You can't be serious.

ALICE. She didn't have a problem taking him from you.

CATHERINE. It was my decision to go to London without him ...

ALICE. Doesn't make it right. Burglary is still burglary if I leave my house unlocked.

CATHERINE. I'm a little shocked, really.

ALICE. Why?

CATHERINE. Because you just sat here and bonded with her over disinterested husbands. Was that an act?

ALICE. I feel for her, but she's not my daughter.

CATHERINE. I see. *(A beat.)* Do you want me to be with him? Porn, pot, no ambition ...

ALICE. He wouldn't have become that man if he'd stayed with you. She's ... She's very sweet, but she's not his equal. You are.

32

Scene 3

Later. Don has come over to Alice's house. He and Catherine are outside (a couple lawn chairs and a grill) drinking beers.

DON. So Gwen tells me she had a spasm of honesty over here today.

CATHERINE. She did.

DON. She does that. *(Opening the grill; postponing the conversation.)* When's the last time someone cleaned this?

CATHERINE. It gets used like once a year.

DON. Then it needs to get cleaned like once a year. *(Starts cleaning the grill.)* Yeah, she does that. And I have to let her because ... She says if I try to muzzle her, she'll start drinking again. Which I'm not convinced would be the worst thing in the world. *(Catherine smiles.)* I just don't think she ever had a problem. You were there. You lived with her ...

CATHERINE. I did.

DON. Did you ever think back then, Gwen's an alcoholic?

CATHERINE. No. I noticed that she could drink more than we could, but I just thought it was ... good genes?

DON. Exactly! Gwen's a New England WASP. Functional alcoholism is her cultural inheritance.

CATHERINE. You think?

DON. Yes. And the WASP way of life ... It's tried and true, everybody stays married.

CATHERINE. The way of life being alcoholism?

DON. Functional alcoholism. They work all day and hate their lives, then they come home and drink martinis for four hours. Then they pass out. You see the wisdom in that setup?

CATHERINE. It sounds like the couple is never interacting sober.

DON. That's right. It's perfect.

CATHERINE. Just to play devil's advocate, wouldn't it be better to create a life that makes you happy so you don't have to drink so much?

DON. Create a life that makes you happy. Sure, that sounds good. How do you do that?

CATHERINE. Do I look like I know?

DON. Hey, you're the one living the dream, right?

CATHERINE. I am?

DON. You're on TV. You're the hot doomsday chick. How'd we get on to this?

CATHERINE. Gwen's spasm of honesty.

DON. Right. So I told Gwen ... I said, if you're gonna go over there and tell them I'm a ... a pot-head, a porn addict, a debtor, a failure ... I have to be able to defend myself.

CATHERINE. That's fair. *(They don't speak for a beat or two.)*

DON. So ... uhh ... pornography.

CATHERINE. Pornography.

DON. What I would like to say on that subject is that the stuff I watch ... You could rent it at a video store in the Eighties. I'm not watching any of the stuff you think is killing us as a culture.

CATHERINE. That's good. Though I probably wouldn't judge you if you were.

DON. Oh, yeah?

CATHERINE. Well ... Do you pay for it?

DON. Hell no. You know how much you can see for free?

CATHERINE. If you're watching the free stuff, you're not even officially a consumer.

DON. You wanna tell Gwen that — I'm not officially a consumer?

CATHERINE. I'm not getting in the middle of your marriage. So it's the porn that bothers you the most? Of all the charges leveled against you today ...

DON. You know my career is shit and I drink too much. All I had left going for me was my sexual dynamism. She had to go and reveal that's gone, too.

CATHERINE. She didn't say it was gone, she said it was redirected to the Internet.

DON. Exactly. She added a dirty raincoat to my already shoddy presentation.

CATHERINE. You don't fall in my estimation because you watch porn.

DON. The stuff I watch is so tame ...

CATHERINE. I believe you. *(A beat, considers the move she then makes.)* But even if it was, like, violent humiliation porn, I'd ... Well, you read my book. I'd agree with Freud that sexual fantasy has both literal and latent content.

DON. Literal and latent content. Hold on, let me dust off the old grad school brain. Aha! You're suggesting that sometimes horny sluts aren't horny sluts; they're symbols. *(She cracks a smile; this is their old dynamic: Don plays literalist to her highfalutin' theory-speak.)*

CATHERINE. You gonna mock me?

DON. Of course, I am.

CATHERINE. I'll give you an example: women who have rape fantasies. Those women don't want really want to be raped. The rape is not a rape —

DON. No, that'd be your literal content.

CATHERINE. Right. A rape fantasy isn't about rape at all. It's the fantasy of sex without responsibility.

DON. Interesting. You think that up?

CATHERINE. No. Nancy Friday wrote about it in the Eighties. If you look at the first generation post-women's movement, ask them their fantasies — *(Stopping herself.)* This stuff is all in my first book. You didn't read it, did you? *(A silence that says "no.")* Wow. *(He puts a hand or two on her. He's a flirt and he's good at it.)*

DON. I know. I'm an asshole.

CATHERINE. *(After a beat.)* Did you read my other book?

DON. I ... No. No, I didn't.

CATHERINE. Wow. *(After a beat.)* It hurts my feelings that you didn't read my books. It's kind of devastating, actually.

DON. Well, imagine how I feel. I'm humiliated.

CATHERINE. Can I ask why you didn't read them?

DON. Ummm ... You know me, I'm not a theory guy.

CATHERINE. You're not a theory guy. Are you kidding me?

DON. I appreciate you trying to elevate my porn habit with your ... your Freud and your Nancy Friday, but at the end of the day I think it's just porn. Like I think movies about teenagers getting tortured are just movies about teenagers getting tortured. When you go on TV and say they're geopolitical critiques of American interventionism abroad ... I just don't see that. If I could think like you think, my life would be very different. But I'm simple folk ... *(She stares, not letting him off the hook.)*

CATHERINE. By "what I do" you mean use academic theory to elevate low art forms. I'm aware you think what I do is bullshit.

DON. I do think it's bullshit. But I've always thought that! That's what made us tick back when we ticked. I haven't done so well without that friction, maybe. I don't know.

CATHERINE. The look in your eyes when you're discrediting my ideas? That is the most alive you've looked since I've been here.

DON. Oh, yeah?

CATHERINE. What happened?

DON. What do you mean?

CATHERINE. You don't teach anymore.

DON. Dean pays better.

CATHERINE. But your passion was teaching.

DON. Yeah, but you know this business.

CATHERINE. What do you mean?

DON. Coming out of school … You know, I didn't get the gigs you got.

CATHERINE. You got the job at Hamden.

DON. I was just adjuncting at Hamden. I made about fifteen grand a year. With a wife and kid.

CATHERINE. You couldn't get a full-time position?

DON. I got one eventually. At a technical college. God, was that grim — sweatshop workload, math geeks who didn't like to read. I got promoted to dean there, which put me on the dean track, got me this gig. More money, better school. In your mother's backyard which is weird, but … a good deal. I mean, it's a fourth-rate liberal arts college. But the kids are nice. They know where they stand.

CATHERINE. You were in a tough position coming out of school …

DON. Yeah, I was a white guy who wanted to teach other white guys. Your Melville, your Whitman …

CATHERINE. You had a soft spot for Emily Dickinson.

DON. Still do. The point is, a thousand other guys wanted to teach American Lit. But how many hot females were writing about porn and torture?

CATHERINE. I had a more unique presentation, that's absolutely true.

DON. You played the game, I didn't.

CATHERINE. I told you fifteen years ago you should write your anti-theory manifesto.

DON. It's been done.

CATHERINE. Not by you.

DON. I guess.

CATHERINE. I just think you should be teaching. Back in school, whenever the undergrads rated their TAs —

DON. Beat your ass every time. Those kids loved me.

CATHERINE. You have a gift. *(This is now getting uncomfortable for Don. Feels like pity.)*

DON. It's not a tragedy. I've got a pretty cush deal here. I don't work much.

CATHERINE. So write your anti-theory book.

DON. My drive's sorta … gone. It's been gone. Sometimes I think I only had it when I was competing with you.

CATHERINE. You have a family. It's a lot easier to be driven when you have no attachments.

DON. Maybe. You think you got where you are because you didn't get married?

CATHERINE. Did I say that?

DON. You said that's maybe a message women get. You have all these opportunities now, don't get bogged down with men.

CATHERINE. I didn't consciously opt out of marriage. I don't think I did. Do you think I did?

DON. I can recall at least one blowout between us about it.

CATHERINE. About marriage?

DON. About whether or not you were gonna get bogged down with a guy. Me being the guy.

CATHERINE. When I left for London, we were good.

DON. Right, but then I asked you to come home and you wouldn't.

CATHERINE. Don, it was only for a year —

DON. Year's a long time for a twenty-five-year-old guy.

CATHERINE. You could have come to me in London as easily as I could drop out, fly home —

DON. Babe, I was rejected for that London fellowship. You know that. You could come home, re-enroll here. If I went to London with you, I'm serving fish 'n' chips — *(Stopping himself.)* Well, there's no point.

CATHERINE. You've done some thinking about this.

DON. Oh, so have you. Your life goes to hell, I'm the guy you're calling drunk after however the fuck many years.

CATHERINE. So now that we've established Gwen can't keep a secret, what did I say that night I called?

DON. You said you had some kind of a bar pick-up go bad and you needed to get out of New York.

CATHERINE. This was right after Mom's heart attack. I was on, like, a vodka IV.

DON. So what happened?

CATHERINE. I picked up a guy in a bar and I woke up, like, the next day.

DON. Better than not waking up.

CATHERINE. I think I was unconscious. I think he choked me.

DON. Oh. I don't think you told Gwen that part.

CATHERINE. I can't believe I just told you that.

DON. You call the police?

CATHERINE. And say what?

DON. I don't know … Someone tried to choke me to death?

CATHERINE. No. I think I asked him to do it.

DON. Oh.

CATHERINE. I mean, I don't know that I did, but I think …

DON. You got your literal and your latent all mixed up. It happens.

CATHERINE. Why did I tell you that?

DON. At least your sexual depravity has a little cachet to it.

CATHERINE. It does?

DON. Picking up a guy in a bar … It's retro. It's cute.

CATHERINE. Why is it retro?

DON. You're supposed to do that stuff on Craigslist now. You're out *Looking for Mr. Goodbar* like it's 1975. I think it's adorable. *(Catherine cracks a smile.)* Whereas my shit is … I'm jerking off to a computer while my family watches *Toy Story*. It's just appalling.

CATHERINE. Still think I'm living the dream?

DON. Oh, it's all … messy. The sex thing. If you don't shut it off when you hit forty, it's gonna get messy. *(A beat.)* Well, this didn't go as planned. I came over to minimize the damage.

CATHERINE. Why do you care what I think of you at this point?

DON. I'm a guy, I've got the caveman wiring.

CATHERINE. What does that mean?

DON. The girl is supposed to cook the big game after I catch it. She's not supposed to catch the big bison instead of me.

CATHERINE. You think I caught the big bison?

DON. You did. And Gwen knows I have my stupid caveman thing about seeing you again on unequal footing. She could have kept her mouth shut for once.

CATHERINE. Here I've been feeling on unequal footing with you because I have no family.

DON. A family's easier to get than a career like yours.

CATHERINE. I don't know that that's true.

DON. Did you want one — a family?

CATHERINE. I would say yes, but ... I think I wanted a family like you wanted a career. I wanted it but I didn't do the stuff you gotta do to get it. *(A beat. He makes some subtle physical move that suggests he'd fool around if she responded.)* Don't do it.

DON. Well ... I have to try.

CATHERINE. No, you do not have to try. If I had come back from London when you asked, would we be married now? *(He thinks on it.)*

DON. If I'm honest ... No. You work harder and you're a couple IQ points smarter. I wouldn't have stuck around for that.

CATHERINE. I think that's very sad.

DON. It is. I was at my best when I was with you. Now look at me. *(A beat.)* I wouldn't blow it now, you know? Now? I'd suck it up, go to therapy, do whatever I had to do to, you know ... be your number two. *(A beat.)* I'm sorry I didn't have this groping towards wisdom back when we could have used it. I'm sorry. *(He starts kissing her.)*

CATHERINE. Don't. Don't do that ... It's too late. We can't just ... Don, stop. It's too late.

DON. Is that...? You really want me to stop or is that a little monologue you need to perform so this isn't your fault?

CATHERINE. The second thing. *(She kisses back. It gets hot and heavy.)*

End of Act One

ACT TWO

Scene 1

Alice's living room. The second week of classes. Avery and Gwen sit in silence. Alice enters.

ALICE. She's coming. She's going over her notes one last time.

GWEN. *(To Alice.)* She and Don were out again last night. Late.

ALICE. There's just so much catching up to do …

GWEN. Still. Three nights this week … *(Alice exits.)*

AVERY. Wait. They go out drinking without you? That's kind of fucked up.

GWEN. Well, I can't go with them; I don't have a — *(A beat. Avery can fill in the blank.)* I don't drink.

AVERY. You don't have a babysitter. I know. *(A beat.)* Have you even tried to find another babysitter? Do you *want* something to happen? *(Catherine rushes in, Alice trailing.)*

CATHERINE. I'm sorry. I'm so sorry.

GWEN. Rough morning, huh? You and Don had some more drinking to do.

CATHERINE. We're still catching up. But I've had time to prepare.

ALICE. What are you discussing today? Should I stay?

CATHERINE. We're discussing torture horror and sadistic pornography.

ALICE. Then I'll see you in an hour to make the drinks. *(Alice leaves.)*

CATHERINE. OK! So let's get started. We'll start with horror movies and then segue into pornography. That sound OK?

GWEN. Delightful.

CATHERINE. All right. I'll give you my little Horror 101 lecture to sort of contextualize the movies we're going to discuss.

GWEN. I wasn't able to make it through the movies you asked us to watch.

CATHERINE. That's OK. Torture horror is not for the faint of heart.

GWEN. I have children. *(A weird, awkward beat.)*

CATHERINE. I know.

AVERY. Why didn't you watch after they went to bed?

GWEN. I tried, but it still felt like bringing pollution into my home.

CATHERINE. It's not a problem.

GWEN. We were talking the other day about Betty Friedan and women being homemakers … How it's not for every woman, but for those who do it … it's a job. Creating a home. *(Another awkward beat.)*

CATHERINE. Well — again — it's fine if you didn't watch the movies. I provided plot summaries for just that reason. So! Why study horror movies? Avery, want to help me out here?

AVERY. Yeah. Basically every generation has anxieties that are unique to them. Like I gather from the reading that your generation was all freaked out about Russia dropping a nuclear bomb? And that … I mean, that means nothing to me.

CATHERINE. Right. Horror movies can be read as the collective nightmares of the generations that produced them. Avery, can you give us an example?

AVERY. Yeah. After World War II, there was all this science fiction horror.

CATHERINE. Yes. Post-World War II, you have great anxiety about scientific advances — *Invasion of the Body Snatchers*, *The Incredible Shrinking Man*. The next trend worth tracking happens around the Vietnam War, and this is the rise of the disaster movie … movies about average joes trapped in a catastrophe not of their making. Movies like *Airport* and *The Towering Inferno*. The Vietnam parallel should be obvious …

GWEN. Should it?

CATHERINE. I think so. There was a draft in effect; the people fighting the war didn't choose to be there. And it's a disaster.

GWEN. Oh. OK.

CATHERINE. So! 1973! Very big year. Richard Nixon pulls the last troops out of Vietnam and the courts pass Roe v. Wade, legalizing abortion. Both houses have passed the Equal Rights Amendment. It still needs to be ratified, but it's been passed. Men are returning from Vietnam to a society where women are empowered as never before. The next wave in horror arrives circa 1977, and it is …

AVERY. The slasher movie!

CATHERINE. Yes. Avery, want to summarize?

AVERY. Yeah, the trend starts when the movie *Halloween* makes a b'jillion dollars in 1978.

CATHERINE. Yes. *Halloween* provides the template for all the slasher movies that follow. Gwen, can you give us the template?

GWEN. It's a woman alone … doing things females traditionally did not do.

CATHERINE. Like?

GWEN. Like casual sex or traveling alone.

AVERY. And working. Usually the women are working … Like they're babysitters. Or camp counselors.

CATHERINE. That's right! So the cultural anxiety that birthed the slasher film should be pretty clear. Film critics at the time condemned these movies as an angry reaction to the women's movement.

AVERY. It's weirdly like … Like Phyllis Schlafly could have made all these movies.

CATHERINE. Why do you say that?

AVERY. Well, she totally threatened women that, if they didn't stay home being housewives, bad shit would happen. These movies just take it a step further, like … Not only will men not protect you, they're gonna fucking kill you.

CATHERINE. Yes, there is a way in which these movies present a grotesque exaggeration of everything Schlafly feared for the liberated woman.

GWEN. You said yourself you don't necessarily disagree with her.

CATHERINE. With Schlafly? I disagree with her politically, but —

GWEN. But you said the other day, you see some validity in her fears for the single career woman.

CATHERINE. Well, I think I had a little spasm of self-disclosure the other day.

AVERY. *(Aimed at Gwen.)* We all did.

GWEN. I don't think Schlafly was threatening women. I think it was more a caution that if you reject the sphere of family and home, your life will be different than your mother's life and … you might not like it.

AVERY. That's a threat.

GWEN. No, it's advice. It's … If you thumb your nose at being a homemaker … Then you'd just better hope what you gave all that up for was worth it. *(Ouch. Very awkward beat. Catherine is thrown; Avery tries to get things back on track.)*

AVERY. I would like to talk about September 11th and the rise of torture horror.

CATHERINE. Terrific. Do you want to, um, tell me what you … what you read …

AVERY. Yeah. Basically, September 11th happened and we went to war, and the horror movies we coughed up to deal with that are … It's torture horror.

CATHERINE. Yes. So one might ask, you know, why slasher movies after Vietnam and torture movies after Iraq?

GWEN. I think what distinguishes the torture film from the slasher film is that the victim is doing something wrong.

CATHERINE. What do you mean?

GWEN. Well, I just read the plot summaries, but these movies are about Americans who go to foreign countries and misbehave. So the people of those countries punish them. Unlike the women in the slasher movies, these victims — these interlopers — are wrong. *(Another awkward beat.)*

AVERY. I disagree with the term "interloper." In *Hostel* the victims are backpacking in Eastern Europe; in *Turistas* it's, like, spring break in Brazil. The "interlopers" in these films are tourists. These countries invited them in.

GWEN. Yes, but an invitation is not carte blanche to do whatever you want. These people behave with such appalling disregard for their hosts …

AVERY. Gwen, you didn't watch any of the movies.

GWEN. Yes, but I have an opinion!

AVERY. The girl in *Turistas* took a picture without asking permission. And the Brazilians harvested her organs.

GWEN. *(Starts to lose it.)* She didn't ask permission! *(A beat.)* All I'm saying is that an invitation is not permission and choices have consequences. *(A beat.)* That's all Schlafly was saying, you know, was … If you decide to stay single and fabulous, you have to live with the consequences. What if you wake up one day and decide … My books don't love me; my degrees and awards don't love me; the five hundred men I've had sex with don't love me … Only my mother loves me, but she — at some point — has to die. Schlafly's point is not that harm will come to that woman, it's that she better have the guts to live with her choices. Own your own misspent life. Don't victimize women who made the other choice. Don't be a thug breaking into a house to steal a TV … oh, my God!

CATHERINE. Let's stop for today.

GWEN. I'm sorry. I just can't ... *(Leaping up; leaving.)* I have to go. *(A beat.)*

AVERY. You're crying.

CATHERINE. Yeah ...

AVERY. You don't have a misspent life.

CATHERINE. Oh, I might.

AVERY. Can we have a martini and talk about it?

CATHERINE. I don't think that's a good idea.

AVERY. OK. But I just want to say ... I think when TVs get stolen, it's usually because the owner left the door open.

CATHERINE. No ... No, Avery, an open door is not permission to steal someone's TV.

AVERY. OK. Maybe you shouldn't steal it, maybe you should just borrow it and use it and teach its owner a lesson.

Scene 2

Alice's living room. Later that evening. Catherine, Gwen, and Don meet to discuss their situation.

GWEN. I take responsibility for my indiscretion. I went to a meeting after I left class today and I shared what happened ...

DON. You atoned for your indiscretion with more indiscretion.

GWEN. Don, the group is anonymous —

DON. We live in a fucking college town, Gwen. I'll bet half the people there know me —

GWEN. They told me I was wrong.

DON. What did you tell them?

GWEN. I said that I had divulged intimate details of my marriage and my husband retaliated by committing an infidelity.

DON. Great. That's fucking great.

GWEN. They told me I was wrong! *(To Catherine.)* In AA we say, "You're only as sick as your secrets," which I thought meant ... If venting is what you need to do to stay sober, do it. And they told me that was wrong.

44

DON. I think I've been telling you that for over a decade …

GWEN. I want this to never have happened, and I think we can go back. If we're all sorry, we can go back.

DON. I'm not sorry.

CATHERINE. Did you two not talk to each other before coming over here?

DON. No, we didn't. But we haven't talked either. I mean, we were up all night —

GWEN. You know what? Have your talk. I'm gonna get some air … *(Gwen exits.)*

CATHERINE. Don, this is not how this works.

DON. How what works?

CATHERINE. Cheating.

DON. Well, we've never done it before; we're new. What happens next?

CATHERINE. Next? I think we apologize and we try to go back. I wish things were different, but they're not.

DON. What does that mean?

CATHERINE. It means … Maybe we wish we'd made different choices in the past, but … we're here now. You have a family and it's too late.

DON. We can't have an affair. I agree that's not right.

CATHERINE. OK. So we'll just all apologize and —

DON. I'm gonna get a divorce.

CATHERINE. What?!

DON. I can't do it anymore. These last couple weeks with you, I feel like a human being again. *(Gwen reenters with momentum.)*

GWEN. I need to disclose something.

DON. More? You have more to disclose?

GWEN. *(To Catherine.)* Are you pretending you don't remember that drunk phone call you made to us?

CATHERINE. I know I told you about picking up men … in bars …

GWEN. We talked about switching.

CATHERINE. What do you mean, "switching"?

GWEN. You said you wanted my life. You said Don was the one who got away and you regretted not having a family. I said I had a fantasy of Julian and me moving to New York. I would finish school while he pursued acting. I said maybe we should switch places and you said, "Like in a Disney movie?" We laughed it off, but the next day I put you on Don's to-do list. I brought you here. I made this happen.

CATHERINE. So you ... You want to switch lives with me?

GWEN. I thought I did, you know? That night you called, Don was on the computer watching porn and I just thought, you know, *take him.* I felt that way right up until you slept together. When that happened, it just threw a switch in me that made me want to keep him. So the point is ... I'm owning that I opened the door. I opened it, and I own that, but now I'm closing it. I changed my mind. OK?

DON. Gwen, are you listening to yourself?

GWEN. I'm taking responsibility.

DON. You are talking about me like I'm a pair of shoes.

GWEN. No, I'm not.

DON. It's like you gave her some old shoes you didn't want, then when she wore them, they started looking good to you again.

GWEN. I had a lapse in judgment, but I have reconnected with my priorities.

DON. Gwen, I'm a goddamn human being.

GWEN. Oh, what is that supposed to mean?

DON. Forget love, forget attraction. There is no aspect of my person that you even like at this point.

GWEN. There are actions you need to take to earn my approval. I deserve —

DON. I know what you deserve, but I can't ... I'm like a fucking dying plant, Gwen. I am withering in the black, sunless hell of your disapproval.

GWEN. You're withering? I could use a little sunlight, too, Don.

DON. Great. We're in agreement; we're killing each other. Let's split.

GWEN. Oh, I see. You're playing hooky from real life, so I'm just supposed to —

DON. *(Overlapping.)* You wanted this to happen! Now it's happened and it's like ... You're like the wimpy kid at the pool who climbs up the ladder, then can't jump off the high dive. You got here. Now jump. Go to New York.

GWEN. I can't do that.

CATHERINE. Why?

GWEN. Why?

CATHERINE. I have an apartment sitting empty there.

GWEN. I have a three-year-old.

CATHERINE. We can take care of him.

GWEN. That's not realistic.

CATHERINE. It is. We could take care of Devon. I could make a call ... get you into summer school in New York. I have friends in theatre. I could find something for Julian, too.

DON. Do it.

GWEN. With what money?

CATHERINE. Mine. Borrow it. Take it. I don't care; I want this.

GWEN. But ... Devon ...

DON. Come back on weekends. It's the twenty-first century. Be a weekend mom.

GWEN. (Now weighing it for real.) No, it's just not realistic.

DON. No. Here's what's not realistic. Thirteen years of you whining about the life you would have had if you weren't saddled with me. I am unsaddling you. Go get happy.

Scene 3

Alice's living room. A week later (the third week of classes; second week in July). Avery has come for class. She sits alone. Catherine enters.

CATHERINE. Hi. Sorry. I'm late. Did Mom let you in?

AVERY. Yeah. Do we still have a class?

CATHERINE. Yes. Gwen won't be back, but we'll keep going.

AVERY. So it's like an independent study now?

CATHERINE. Yeah, is that all right?

AVERY. It's great. Are you ... Did you just have sex?

CATHERINE. What? No! I just ... I rushed. From upstairs. (A beat. There's no point in lying; Avery knows.)

AVERY. I think it's great.

CATHERINE. Really?

AVERY. Yeah! Have a hot summer affair. I think that's awesome.

CATHERINE. Actually, it's more than an affair ... (Don enters. He and Catherine interact like new lovers — beaming, touching, etc.)

DON. Hey, Cathy ... Oh! Hey, Avery. What's shakin'?

47

AVERY. I don't know, Dean Harper, you tell me.

DON. I'm gonna go get another load of my stuff. Can I take those two closets in the guest room?

CATHERINE. Yeah, yeah, do it.

DON. I'm thinking we make that Devon's room. That sound right?

CATHERINE. Yeah, will he go for it? I don't want to leave my mom.

DON. No, I know. I'll bring him over; we'll make it work. *(Don leaves. Avery reacts with alarm. Can she talk Catherine out of this before he moves his stuff in?)*

AVERY. Wait. He's moving in?

CATHERINE. He is.

AVERY. With Devon?

CATHERINE. Gwen is going to take Julian to New York for the rest of the summer and stay at my place. If they're happy there, we'll make this all ... permanent.

AVERY. Are you kidding me?

CATHERINE. I know it sounds crazy ...

AVERY. Why don't you just fuck him for the summer, then give him back?

CATHERINE. Because I ... love him. Avery, I think this is why none of my relationships in the last fifteen years have worked. Don was the one. My one. You don't look happy for me.

AVERY. I am. I just ... I mean, I babysat for them.

CATHERINE. Right.

AVERY. I've seen your future should you choose to accept it.

CATHERINE. Meaning ...

AVERY. Don is all about not expending energy. If he moves his stuff in, you're gonna be stuck with him.

CATHERINE. I want to be stuck with him.

AVERY. OK, but ... I don't know how much experience you have with guys who, like, smoke pot every day and watch porn. Was he like that when you dated him?

CATHERINE. He smoked a little. And porn ... I don't think so.

AVERY. I would just say that the whole Internet porn thing can be really tied up in the whole pot/low ambition thing. Does that make sense?

CATHERINE. Avery, I know he's not a go-getter.

AVERY. Not a go-getter? The only reason he has a job is because Gwen is on his ass every minute not to slack.

CATHERINE. Right. And I think she's beaten him down. Don was never ambitious, but he had passion once ...

AVERY. He doesn't anymore. Do you want Gwen's life? Do you want your life to be nagging about money and giving ultimatums about porn?

CATHERINE. I don't need him to make a lot of money. And as far as porn ... I mean, maybe that's not a big deal breaker for me. You don't think porn's a big deal —

AVERY. I don't think it's, like, immoral, but I'm not gonna be happy if my man chooses it over me.

CATHERINE. So it's either/or — sex and porn? Men don't do both? Oh, my God. I'm twice your age. It humiliates me to be talking to you like this.

AVERY. Like what?

CATHERINE. Like I'm a child asking where babies come from.

AVERY. It's OK. I think once you go down the porn road and give up the real thing, it's hard to go back. It's like ... once you start getting directions from Google, it seems like a huge hassle to unfold a map. Does that make sense?

CATHERINE. Yes.

AVERY. And if it winds up, like, you make all the money and he almost never has sex with you ... I mean, what do you get out of that?

CATHERINE. Love?

AVERY. You can get that from girls, though. I don't mean lesbians, I mean ... If you need someone to be sweet when you have a bad day ... I kind of think that's what girlfriends are for.

CATHERINE. Really?

AVERY. My mom says the only deal breakers in marriage are money and sex. Which to me means like ... The emotional stuff you can outsource if he's pulling his weight with the money and the sex.

CATHERINE. Avery, I don't think you can outsource love.

AVERY. Why?

CATHERINE. You're young. Your parents are healthy. There will come a day when that's not the case and then ... I don't think a person should be alone to face the things you have to face between middle-age and death. And I don't think friends are enough, Avery. I think that's what romantic love is for. *(Off Avery's look.)* You don't agree.

AVERY. Honestly? Here's what I think "love" is. You know how

49

when you get drunk you get nicer? Like I'll get drunk and decide some annoying girl is my new best friend. I'll smoke a hundred cigarettes with her and bond like we're at camp and then ... when I sober up, she just seems annoying again and I'm stuck having brunch with her. You know?

CATHERINE. I do.

AVERY. Drunk is your body under the influence of alcohol and "love" is your body under the influence of hormones. Booze, sex hormones ... they do the same thing, which is dupe you into thinking average people are great.

CATHERINE. What a grim philosophy.

AVERY. I'm a Bio major. Evolutionarily? It makes total sense. The love-drunk lasts about six months. Just enough time to get knocked up and trapped. *(Alice enters.)*

ALICE. Would it be terrible to have our drink a little early today? I don't want to be drinking when Don's little boy gets here ...

CATHERINE. We haven't started class ...

AVERY. We'll start now.

ALICE. I'll make the drinks. *(Alice leaves. Avery can see that Catherine's troubled by what she's said.)*

CATHERINE. OK. Today we're supposed to cover reality television and the death of privacy. That was all Gwen's assignment.

AVERY. Fucking Gwen, man.

CATHERINE. But reality TV ... That's your area, right?

AVERY. I don't know if it is anymore.

CATHERINE. Really? Why?

AVERY. Umm ... Lucas is in L.A. for the summer interning for a producer and ... *(Is there a face-saving way to word this?)* He's big-time hanging out with a girl. I don't know if they're hooking up or not.

CATHERINE. I'm sure he's not hooking up. You're exclusive, right?

AVERY. He better be hooking up with her. If he's not, I'm definitely screwed.

CATHERINE. Wait. It's better if he's sleeping with her?

AVERY. If he's just hooking up, then it'll end. If they're, like, connecting with hearts and minds ... Then I'm fucked. *(A beat.)* I've been thinking about the other day ... about your mom saying men won't buy a cow they're already milking? Why would that be? Why would they punish us for giving them what they want?

CATHERINE. I've spent twenty-five years trying to win this

argument with my mother.

AVERY. And?

CATHERINE. You mentioned evolution ...

AVERY. Right ...

CATHERINE. Let's think caveman. A caveman wants a woman who will bear his children and stay by his campfire. If a cavewoman gives him sex too easily ... Maybe he has to worry she's not campfire material.

AVERY. You can't like sex and campfires?

CATHERINE. Maybe his fear is if you give sex too easily ... Once the love-drunk passes, you'll be on to another campfire.

AVERY. That is so heavy. You're saying that we still mate like cave people.

CATHERINE. I think it's a possibility. *(A painful silence.)*

AVERY. The girl Lucas is hanging out with is Mormon. Like, the real deal; she's a fucking consultant on a movie about Mormons. So they're definitely not hooking up, and he's stopped calling me. I've lost him. To a Mormon. *(Don rushes in. He's holding a leaf. It's a striking leaf, to be sure. Half is green and new, the other half has turned brown.)*

DON. I'm really leaving this time, but you gotta see this ...

CATHERINE. What is it?

DON. It's a leaf! *(A beat. They all look at the leaf.)*

CATHERINE. Look at that ...

DON. It's half summer, half fall. You see that? It's half alive, half dead.

AVERY. Heavy.

DON. The leaf is a message.

CATHERINE. What's the message?

DON. The leaf says ... It says get your kicks while you can, children. Summer's half over.

Scene 4

Alice's living room; sunrise. A month later, getting towards mid-August. Don and Cathy have been up all night. He's in pajama bottoms only, holding a beer and maybe a bag of chips. She's in a nightie or slip and also has a beer. Neither is drunk or even tipsy, just beer-mellow. The room is noticeably less tidy — not trashed, just enough disorder and debris to suggest lazy lovers hanging out over weeks. The pair is physically close, affectionate. (In the transition to this scene, maybe Don and Cathy strip to their underwear and slowly mess up the room while lazy/sexy groovy music plays — something like The Brian Jonestown Massacre's "Let's Pretend It's Summer." *)

CATHERINE. I love this.

DON. What?

CATHERINE. Watching the sun come up ... still a little bit drunk ...

DON. The sun is a little bit drunk?

CATHERINE. Misplaced modifier, I know.

DON. See? Spend a month with me, you relax all your standards. Moral, grammatical, nutritional ...

CATHERINE. My standards needed relaxing.

DON. *(Re: the beer.)* Should we have one more?

CATHERINE. There aren't any more.

DON. I bought two six-packs.

CATHERINE. We started drinking at dinner.

DON. Huh. OK. What about the pizza?

CATHERINE. It's out there. It's cold.

DON. Right.

CATHERINE. You want to do a pizza breakfast? Why not? I could go for that.

DON. We should probably switch to coffee. Devon and your mom will be up soon.

CATHERINE. I was thinking we could go back to bed for a

while. Mom's always offering to watch Devon so we can sleep in.

DON. No, he's too much for her. I'll take him.

CATHERINE. They did a puzzle the other day for almost an hour. He's actually very gentle with her.

DON. Yeah ... I feel like I gotta redeem myself, you know? Take a shower, eat a vegetable. If I let the debauchery go past sunrise, it messes with my self-respect.

CATHERINE. OK. I actually asked Avery to come by and help Mom. With Devon. I thought it might be nice to get some sleep. Maybe over at your place ... *(Alice enters.)*

ALICE. Are we up early or did we not go to bed?

CATHERINE. We did a film festival.

ALICE. A film festival?

DON. You pick a filmmaker ... Start at like eight o'clock, watch all their movies, or as many as you can, all the way through 'til morning.

ALICE. That sounds like fun.

CATHERINE. I don't know about "fun"; it was a Bergman festival.

ALICE. Bergman ... He has the man playing chess with death, right?

DON. Very good! You're a Bergman fan?

ALICE. No. Whenever Cathy sees a movie she calls and tells me all about it. Then I don't have to go.

DON. You don't like to go to the movies? God, if I was you ... retired ... I'd go every day. You should go!

ALICE. Go by myself, you mean?

CATHERINE. She won't do it; I've tried. *(To Alice.)* We didn't get to the chess-with-death movie. *(From upstairs, we hear something hit the floor.)*

CATHERINE. What was that?

ALICE. That's Devon throwing the alarm clock. It's our new little routine. Can I go get him dressed?

DON. Go for it.

ALICE. I'm just a little bit in love with him ... *(Alice leaves. A beat.)*

CATHERINE. You know what? You're right. When the sun comes up, we should clean up our act. *(A beat.)* Did you ... talk to Gwen about the conference?

DON. Conference. The Italian thing?

CATHERINE. My Dario Argento lecture. I really want you to go with me. It's in Florence; it's going to be beautiful.

DON. I don't know if I can take a week off, though.

CATHERINE. It's winter break. Remember?

DON. That's right. I gotta run it by Gwen.

CATHERINE. They just need to know. These conferences are like weddings; everything's booked months in advance.

DON. I'll call Gwen. Do you have to say Dario Argento is a genius because you're in his homeland?

CATHERINE. I will be saying that, yes. *(A beat.)* Call her now? She's up early, right?

DON. Yeah. *(Catherine kisses him and leaves. Don picks up the phone and calls Gwen. On the phone.)* Hey. It's me. *(Pause.)* We did stay up all night, yeah. Are you — *(Pause.)* Bergman. *(Pause.)* No, I'm gonna watch Devon. The women are just getting him dressed. Any other questions? *(Pause.)* I'm great. How are you? *(Pause.)* Uh-huh. *(Pause.)* Sure. *(Pause.)* Uh-huh. No, I heard you; you're the oldest kid in the class. *(Pause.)* I don't know. I guess if it bothers you that much, you should quit. *(Pause.)* Refund or no refund … I mean, I don't think Catherine's really sweating the money. *(Pause.)* I don't know where she gets it. I think it's speaking … lectures … *(Pause; she's said something that amuses him.)* People will pay to see a pretty girl talk dirty; that's true. So … The reason I'm calling is — *(Longer pause.)* OK. I mean, do what you want, but … If you come back here, where does that leave Julian? *(Pause.)* Gwen, you can't drag him home now; he's having the time of his life. You can come home without him — *(Pause.)* Because he's more mature than either of us, that's why. If you're unhappy, come home. Let him stay. *(Catherine and Alice enter. Catherine motions that they'll leave if Don needs privacy, but he doesn't. He winks at her and pats the seat next to him on the couch. So she joins him. Alice takes another seat. On the phone.)* The birthday? *(He sighs; pause.)* I did think about it. I think we gotta let 'em go. Both of them. I'm sorry to say that, but … *(Pause.)* Nope. That's all I got. Talk to you soon. *(Don disconnects his call.)* Where's Dev?

ALICE. He's staged some kind of stuffed animal war.

CATHERINE. He's happy. What's wrong with Gwen?

DON. A variety of things.

CATHERINE. Like …

DON. She's the oldest chick in that class you got her into. So she's having a complex. Julian, though ... I forgot to tell you this. Julian's been showing up at every performance of *Wicked*. They do a lottery for front row seats. He went twenty, thirty times, and then he won.

CATHERINE. Wow!

DON. That's not the best part. He met this little Goth cutie hanging out on the line. Kid's got himself a girlfriend.

CATHERINE. Isn't Julian gay?

DON. All signs were pointing in that direction.

CATHERINE. The biggest one being ... showing up to thirty performances of *Wicked*.

DON. Gwen's freaking out.

CATHERINE. Because he's straight?

DON. Because he's not hanging out with her.

ALICE. He's almost fourteen.

DON. And Devon's turning four next week, and she had this big party planned. Now it looks like neither of our kids wants to be there.

ALICE. Where does Devon want to be?

DON. Devon's got this townie redneck pal, Anthony, who has his same birthday. Anthony invited him to *Monster Trucks* that night.

CATHERINE. What are you gonna do?

DON. It's up to Gwen. I told her the party's for the kids, not us; if they don't want it ... She knows I'm right, but she's weepy about it.

CATHERINE. Did you ask her about Italy?

DON. Nah, it sorta felt like kickin' her when she's down.

CATHERINE. Sure. The organizer just needs an answer —

DON. Cathy, I'm not gonna beat one out of her when she's crying. *(Tension. Alice feels she should leave.)*

ALICE. *(Rising.)* I'm going to start the coffee.

DON. I gotta go home. To my house. I'll take Devon with.

CATHERINE. What do you have to do at your house?

DON. Just ... troubleshoot. I'm losing an instructor. Guy's mother died; he has to run home to ... Kansas? Might be Kentucky. I gotta find someone to step in, finish his course.

CATHERINE. *(Straddling him.)* If you really don't want to go to Italy, you can tell me.

DON. I want to.

CATHERINE. Really? *(He kisses her quickly, then lifts her off of him.)*

DON. I do. I just gotta run home ... *(Don gets up. Catherine stops him.)*

55

CATHERINE. Hey, can I just show you something first?

DON. Sure. *(Catherine gets up and retrieves a piece of paper from a desk. She gives it to Don, then snuggles up.)*

CATHERINE. This is a review ... of a book which is getting a ridiculous amount of attention.

DON. *(Reading.)* A Fish Story for Warriors.

CATHERINE. This guy teaches at Penn. He spent a year doing book clubs with guys coming back from Iraq and Afghanistan. He had them read *Moby-Dick* ...

DON. Uh-huh.

CATHERINE. And his shtick is sort of ... He'd read the novel and taught it for twenty years, but these men coming back from war made him look at it differently.

DON. Seems kinda gimmicky.

CATHERINE. Yes! That's my point. All this is is a rip off of that book *Reading Lolita in Tehran* which was, you know, finding new insights into *Lolita* by reading it with Muslim women.

DON. So what ... you want me to read this book?

CATHERINE. No, I want you to write it. This is the kind of book that doesn't take years to write and can really put you on the map in academia.

DON. You want me to start a book club and write a book about it?

CATHERINE. It's just an example.

DON. Yeah, I could do that. I could, like, read *The Scarlet Letter* with knocked up teenagers.

CATHERINE. See, you're joking ... but that is a book you could sell.

DON. Yeah, and I'd get to hang out with teenage sluts.

CATHERINE. Are you mad that I'm showing you this?

DON. No. I don't know if it's really my style, but ... I'll ruminate over it. I guess. Thanks. *(Now, it's feeling awkward.)*

CATHERINE. I just think that ... When we got back together, you said I made you feel, like, aspirational again.

DON. I didn't realize I was on a schedule.

CATHERINE. You're not.

DON. It's summer, Cathy.

CATHERINE. I just want to give you what you need.

DON. Wait. Is this like ... Do you want me to have a book-in-progress I can talk about in Italy?

CATHERINE. No! You just said you wanted to redeem yourself

and I realized … I've been goofing off with you when maybe I should be encouraging you …

DON. I'm sorry. Neither of us have had any sleep …

CATHERINE. I just want you to be happy. *(Don kisses her forehead.)*

DON. We're good. Just … Next time I suggest a film festival, say no. *(Quick kiss on the lips, then Don leaves. Catherine thinks a bit. Then Alice enters.)*

ALICE. Avery's here. She's talking to Don.

CATHERINE. Yeah, he wants to take Devon to his house. Let's just … Tell Avery I'll still pay her.

ALICE. I think Devon has more fun here …

CATHERINE. *(Snapping a little.)* Mother, he's Don's child.

ALICE. Did you two have an argument?

CATHERINE. I think so. *(Avery enters.)*

AVERY. OK, he just left here in his pajamas.

ALICE. Did he take the baby?

AVERY. The baby and a box of pizza. He's so lame. You know he's going over there to smoke a bowl, right?

ALICE. Not in front of Devon!

AVERY. He'll wait 'til nap time. *(To Catherine.)* Your mom filled me in about Gwen. You see what she's doing here, right?

CATHERINE. I think she's having some adjustment pains.

AVERY. Well, yeah. Little miss we-can-switch-places is finding out you can live her life, but she can't live yours. So she's switching strategies. You see that, right?

CATHERINE. No, honestly. I don't.

AVERY. Please. She took copious notes when we discussed Schlafly and Rousseau.

ALICE. And Phil …

AVERY. She can't hack it in New York so she wants back in here. So what's she doing? She is swooning and shaming him. She's un-leashing her fucking siren song of loserness, and she is going to get him back if you don't take control.

ALICE. *(To Avery.)* We've become such a happy family here …

AVERY. I still think he's a loser and you can do better. But if it's really what you want, I can help you.

CATHERINE. It's what I want.

AVERY. OK. Trust me. I have a proven track record —

CATHERINE. With Lucas, you mean?

AVERY. Yes.

CATHERINE. You're back together?

AVERY. I'm not sure yet; he's still in L.A. But I used what I learned in your class and we're talking again.

ALICE. What did you do?

AVERY. I made up a fake crisis about my car and called him for advice. That got him to return my call. After that, I just made sure — in every interaction — to focus on what is not going well in my life.

CATHERINE. Oh, my God … What's happened to you?

AVERY. I'm becoming realistic. It's no good for us to live with integrity while people like Gwen and Lucas' Mormon are manipulating our men.

ALICE. I was thinking that later I might become short of breath and almost fall. I would do this where Don could see me …

CATHERINE. That's a joke, right?

AVERY. *(To Alice.)* Let Don catch you. Tell him you feel safer with a man in the house.

CATHERINE. This is beneath us! All of us!

ALICE. Think of it as building his confidence. That's a loving act.

CATHERINE. Build his confidence! I do nothing else!

AVERY. That's great. What are you doing?

CATHERINE. Well. Just today, for example, I encouraged him to write a book …

AVERY. No!!

ALICE. Cathy, no.

AVERY. You shouldn't have done that.

CATHERINE. I'm confused. I'm losing him to Gwen, but all Gwen does is tell him where he's lacking.

ALICE. That's different.

AVERY. Completely different. *(A beat. Catherine's maddeningly at a loss.)*

CATHERINE. I don't understand!

AVERY. OK, listen to me. When I was little I used to ice skate. And then I stopped. Now when my family watches the Winter Olympics I say, "If I'd kept skating, I could be there." And my mom and dad say, "That's right. If you hadn't quit, you'd be at the Olympics." Do you get it?

CATHERINE. No.

AVERY. I was never going to get to the Olympics. Just like Don was never gonna write books. Just like Gwen is never gonna finish school and have a career. We all have personal mythologies we cherish. The people we love go along with them but understand they are never going to happen. Hence, they do not push us to make them happen.

CATHERINE. Don looked me in the eyes and said, "I want to be what I might have been."

AVERY. Was he stoned? That's a stoned thing to say.

ALICE. *(To Avery.)* Surely we can make this work! Catherine makes enough money; she really doesn't need Don to change.

AVERY. You have to convince him he can be your man just the way he is.

CATHERINE. I tried accepting him the way he his. He didn't like it.

AVERY. Oh, no ... What did you do?

CATHERINE. I don't want to ... My mother is here.

ALICE. Cathy, what did you do?

CATHERINE. I tried ... I tried to watch porn with him.

AVERY. You have to call me before you do stuff like that.

CATHERINE. You just said I should accept him the way he is.

AVERY. Right, but that's not who he is. Don is not a highly evolved superfreak; he's just a stoner who likes porn. Again, you tried to get him to be something he's not. When you do that to a man, you emasculate him.

CATHERINE. OK. OK, I see.

AVERY. The next thing we have to discuss is ... this. *(Re: Cathy's nightie, the beer, etc.)* What you're doing now ... drinking all night, eating garbage, day-sleeping in your own filth. No man wants that from a woman. A man wants his woman to be a civilizing influence.

CATHERINE. *(A horrible realization.)* You read more Schlafly. You read more than I assigned!

AVERY. I have, and I'm seeing results.

ALICE. Please listen to Avery.

AVERY. Schlafly. It's time to listen to Schlafly.

Scene 5

A week later. Don and Gwen's backyard as in the first scene, only now there's a sheet cake on the table. It's decorated with all sorts of vehicles. Don and Gwen sit looking at the cake.

GWEN. I forgot to cancel the cake. It's just so big and I didn't know who else to call.

DON. *(Re: the cake.)* Is that a backhoe?

GWEN. The girl at the bakery didn't know what a backhoe looked like so I took her Devon's book.

DON. *Vehicles?*

GWEN. Yep. *Vehicles.*

DON. He was looking for that.

GWEN. It was at the bakery.

DON. It's a great cake.

GWEN. Thanks.

DON. It was nice of you to invite Catherine and Alice. They're coming later with Avery.

GWEN. Well. Devon loves them. I need to be flexible. *(New thought.)* They all drink so much. I don't have any alcohol.

DON. I got a few beers in the basement.

GWEN. Don, those beers are older than Devon. I put them in the trash and you took them out.

DON. I did.

GWEN. It's disgusting.

DON. I know. *(A beat. This dynamic feels good to both of them.)* So, how ya doin'?

GWEN. Lousy. Mostly about Julian. How is it possible, Don? He sings show tunes —

DON. World's changing, Gwendolyn.

GWEN. What does that mean?

DON. Women are running for president. Men are exfoliating. It's all jumbled; you can't read the signs.

GWEN. I went to a meeting. In New York. They told me that by focusing on the gay/straight question I was avoiding the thing that truly scares me, which is Julian getting an independent life.

DON. Right. *(A beat.)* Couldn't you have figured that out on your own?

GWEN. I went to a group in New York. Nobody knew you.

DON. I'm just saying … do you need it?

GWEN. Yes.

DON. OK.

GWEN. *(After a beat.)* You look like shit, you know. I'm not saying that from a vindictive place; you really don't look good.

DON. My skin, you mean?

GWEN. Your hair is dirty. Yeah, your skin looks bad. You're drinking and eating crap and staying up all night, right?

DON. Pretty much.

GWEN. Does she do all that stuff with you?

DON. Yeah.

GWEN. Wow. You found a woman willing to live like a teenage boy. And she watches horror movies and porn. You must be in pig heaven over there.

DON. You know what it is? It's like first year of college, getting outta my parents' house.

GWEN. Thanks.

DON. You know what I mean. It's a blast 'til it starts disgusting you. Then you gotta kick your own ass and that's … It's hard.

GWEN. It has never been your strength.

DON. *(After a beat.)* She wants me to write a book.

GWEN. Ha! Does she know what a trail of tears that mission's gonna be?

DON. I think she's figuring it out.

GWEN. She ready to send you home?

DON. No, she wants to keep me. Sloth and poverty and all.

GWEN. Well. I guess you got lucky.

DON. I want to come home. Do I have a snowball's chance in hell you'll let me?

GWEN. Of course I'll let you. What are my other options?

DON. No … You have options. Don't think about money. I can go to the Y; I can turn the utility shed out back into like a slave cottage …

GWEN. It's not the money. I want you to come home.

DON. Why?

GWEN. I don't want to date. I don't want to go back to school. I don't even want to find myself on a yoga retreat. I want my old, fucked-up life back.

DON. I want it, too.

GWEN. Don't forget how we got here. I was over at her house crying into my Shirley Temple about how bad our marriage is.

DON. Right. There's stuff I can change, and there's stuff I can't. The porn … I can ditch that. But I would be lying if I sat here and told you I was gonna reinvent myself and make a bunch of money.

GWEN. *(After a beat.)* Oh, I see. She's gonna go back to New York eventually and you don't have the guts to go with her. You don't want to go to cocktail parties full of people with better careers than you.

DON. You're right. I don't. But that's not why I want back in here.

GWEN. You ever see Devon at the park with me? He's scared of the big slide. So when the cool kids go there, he comes and cuddles with me. I only get cuddled when he's too chicken to go down the big slide.

DON. So we're not big slide kinda people. I miss you. I miss my life.

GWEN. I don't know, Don …

DON. Dean Keller is pushing seventy. When he retires, I'll go after his deanship. Be about twenty grand more than I make now. I might not get it …

GWEN. Oh, are we dealing now?

DON. If you want.

GWEN. *(After a beat.)* I mean, I can work on it, but you're probably not coming home to any big … sexual revolution, you know?

DON. I know. *(But they lock eyes long enough and the deal is made. He kisses her on the lips. This is not passion. But could it be? Gwen kisses him again. Keeps kissing him. Avery enters holding a wrapped gift for Devon. Gwen pulls out of the kiss.)*

AVERY. *(To Don.)* They're on their way over here. You need to tell her and not at your kid's birthday party.

Scene 6

Still outside at Don and Gwen's. Later. Don and Catherine alone. Catherine has bought a present for Devon. She tries taking a bright, positive, "We're still OK!" tack ... as if she can defy reality with positivity.

DON. It's my fault. I just ... I got excited and I jumped, you know? I didn't think it all through.

CATHERINE. I think it's my fault ...

DON. No. You're perfect. This is all on me.

CATHERINE. I don't do relationships well, you know. I'm a pusher and —

DON. You are a pusher. And you have a kick-ass life to show for it.

CATHERINE. Well, it's OK for me to push myself, but it's not my place to push you. Or any man.

DON. I don't know if that's true ...

CATHERINE. I will never push you to do anything ever again. You don't have to go to Italy. You don't have to write a book ...

DON. I appreciate that, but —

CATHERINE. *(Remembering Avery's notes.)* I won't push you, but I also won't tolerate ... There will be rigor and routine. No more gluttony, no more sloth ...

DON. Cathy, I have to go home.

CATHERINE. Please don't. *(Quiet. She's totally devastated. He's surprised how devastated.)*

CATHERINE. I really want this to work.

DON. It can't. *(This sinks in.)*

CATHERINE. Tell me why?

DON. It's not worth your time in the analysis. I'm not worth it. You should just curse me and move on.

CATHERINE. I don't want to curse you. I want to understand ... why is this happening? I gave you everything you said you wanted.

DON. You did.

CATHERINE. So...? *(A beat.)*

DON. If I actually articulate this stuff, my low self-esteem will sink to subterranean levels.

CATHERINE. Do it. *(A beat. This is gonna hurt.)*

DON. You look at me like you see lost potential.

CATHERINE. I do.

DON. I don't want to live under that … gaze.

CATHERINE. OK, but I tried no expectations. I said what the hell, it's summer; let's just drink and fuck around …

DON. Yeah, you can't do that with me. I need to be held to a standard or I just sink …

CATHERINE. You're not making sense. Are you saying my expectations were too high or too low?

DON. Both! Gwen holds me to a grade-C achievable standard. Your standards … When they weren't scary high, they were scary low, you know? Gwen and I are … We both want to go back. Go home. *(A beat.)* You look terrified.

CATHERINE. I am. I'm losing my mother and I thought I was gonna have you.

DON. Why would you want me? I'm a charming devil, but am I really who you want on your arm at your next book party?

CATHERINE. Yeah. You are.

DON. *(After a beat.)* You know what I think? I think you're gonna call me from Italy in a few months and thank me. You're gonna meet some hot-shit 30-year-old semiotician with a book on … the Brontë sisters and Norwegian black metal. Your eyes will meet across a piazza and —

CATHERINE. Stop. If you're gonna go home, go home, but don't tell me this is what's best for me — It isn't. You want to fall back on your flawed, tired marriage … Join the fucking club! I want a flawed, tired marriage to cushion my falls. I am ready and willing to embrace mediocrity and ambivalence, you're just not letting me.

DON. *(After a beat.)* I'm sorry. I'm … Hit me? Please. Hit me. *(Catherine puts her hand up to cut him off. She leaves rather than say more.)*

Scene 5

Back home (Alice's living room), lights low. Catherine and Avery sit in silence. Mom hovers nearby.

AVERY. OK, this is my proposal. We go to New York.
CATHERINE. You and me?
AVERY. I'll be your assistant. And we'll do online dating together. We'll fearlessly go in search of men worthy of us.
CATHERINE. Don was worthy.
AVERY. No, he wasn't.
ALICE. He's a good man …
AVERY. A good man? Look what he did to her!
ALICE. He made a mistake. But he had the courage to admit it and set things right before —
CATHERINE. Wow, you are not making this any easier.
ALICE. Cathy, you've been dumped in an email; you've had men disappear without a goodbye. Don did the best he could by you. He apologized.
AVERY. He gets credit for saying he's sorry? Seriously?
ALICE. You're so young. You'll get to an age where that consideration from a man seems quite remarkable.
AVERY. *(After a beat.)* You're right. I'm dumped for a Mormon and Lucas won't even … He's frozen me out. I didn't even get an email making it official.
ALICE. No, Don's a good egg …
CATHERINE. Are you're trying to make me so angry I won't miss you when you're gone? *(Alice goes to Catherine and cuddles close to her.)*
ALICE. Stop thinking about me being gone.
CATHERINE. Both your sisters died within a year of their heart attacks —
ALICE. Well, I'm tougher. What if I promised you two years?
CATHERINE. You can't. You can't always give me what I want.
ALICE. Take Avery back to New York with you. You've got that extra room. You should live like … Oh, one of those sitcoms where girls have adventures. Be *Laverne and Shirley!*

CATHERINE. Laverne and Shirley were factory workers.

ALICE. You know what I mean.

AVERY. Maybe we could find a father and son to date!

ALICE. Oh, that would make a wonderful sitcom!

AVERY. Come on, that would be so fun!

ALICE. Do it. For me.

CATHERINE. I came home to take care of you.

ALICE. Your unhappiness will shorten my life. Go with Avery.

CATHERINE. *(To Avery.)* Don't you have another year of school left?

AVERY. Yeah, but … There is no way I can be on this campus with Lucas if he doesn't want me anymore.

ALICE. You're not very good feminists, you two. Ready to crumble and die over boys.

CATHERINE. *You're* invoking feminism? *(A beat.)*

ALICE. Why don't we all have a martini.

AVERY. God, I would love that.

ALICE. Good! I'll make martinis and you two start hatching your plans. *(As she goes …)* To think of you two loose in New York City! Oh, it could be dangerous! *(On her way out she stops at a "hurricane lamp" — or what Pottery Barn markets as one: a big candle enclosed by glass.)* We'll light the hurricane, too. We'll get all nice and cozy. *(Avery and Catherine don't speak immediately. Catherine gets the lamp. She hunts for matches and finds some. As she lights the candle …)*

AVERY. Are you still thinking about Don?

CATHERINE. No. I was at an academic conference in Virginia a few years ago. And there was a hurricane threatening one of the Carolinas. Two states away, but she — my mother — kept calling me. She was so worried! It was really an irrational fear and I got very annoyed with her. I was just thinking that after she's gone … I could have a husband, I could have a child and … Neither of them would make those calls. You know? No one is ever going to love me that much. I've lived my life alone because I've never been alone.

AVERY. I could be there for you. When your mom dies.

CATHERINE. Thank you, Avery.

AVERY. You don't have to let me live with you.

CATHERINE. I think it's a good idea, actually. I don't want to be alone with myself after this.

AVERY. Me neither! *(After a beat.)* I wrote my final paper. For your class.

CATHERINE. Oh, good.

AVERY. Can I tell you about it?

CATHERINE. Let's wait 'til we have class tomorrow. I'm just —

AVERY. No, I think you should hear it now.

CATHERINE. OK.

AVERY. So in class we talked about slasher movies being an angry reaction to the women's movement. Like, the women started getting independent, so the men freaked out and made all these movies about women being cut up.

CATHERINE. Right …

AVERY. Well, I read this woman Carol Clover's book, and she doesn't agree with you.

CATHERINE. Yeah, Clover has a different take.

AVERY. She says slasher movies invented what she calls the "final girl" — the last surviving girl at the end of the movie who fights for her life and wins. Clover says that character didn't exist before slasher movies. Before slasher movies, a man always came in at the end and saved her.

CATHERINE. Yes. Clover thinks slasher films are actually pro-feminist because the woman is finally allowed to fight her own battle and win.

AVERY. I really like that, you know? When you look at it that way, it's like … OK, maybe the world has changed. That guy who comes in and saves the girl in the end? He might not be coming. But the girl is still gonna be OK.

CATHERINE. *(After a beat.)* Want to go to Italy with me in January?

AVERY. Hell, yes! *(Alice returns with the martini shaker and a glass full of olives.)*

ALICE. Avery, you've seen where I keep the glasses, haven't you?

AVERY. I sure have. *(Avery goes and gets three martini glasses and lines them up. Alice pours the martinis.)*

ALICE. Now, look at that. The hurricane makes everything nice and cozy. We'll have a nice drink by the hurricane and we'll all feel better. And we should toast!

AVERY. Can we do more than one?

ALICE. Yes! We should each make a toast. Who starts?

AVERY. I think we should toast Don and Gwen. Because they're going to need it. We are about to go and seize life by the throat while they're stuck here.

ALICE. That's a wonderful toast! Biting yet generous. *(They clink glasses and drink.)*

CATHERINE. To broken hearts mending. After heart attacks and disappointments in love. May we all … feel better.

ALICE. Oh, that's a good one, too. *(They clink glasses and drink.)*

CATHERINE. Now, you.

ALICE. Oh, goodness. I don't know. *(A beat.)* No, I do. I know! To Phyllis Schlafly!

CATHERINE. What?

ALICE. She said you girls would pay for your independence and your whoring. She said men wouldn't stay with you and she was right. You're free. You're free … *(A beat; Alice thinks of her own life and what might have been …)* I think it's wonderful! *(They clink glasses and drink. Then a silence in which excitement gives way to fear, but not enough to break their resolve.)*

End of Play

PROPERTY LIST

Citronella candles
Hardcover books
Beers
Water
Pen
Class syllabus (3)
Small tray with: martini shaker, olives, Shirley Temple drink
Martini glasses
Grill-cleaning tools
Leaf, half green and half brown
Bag of chips
Phone
Paper
Sheet cake decorated with vehicles
Hurricane lamp
Matches

SOUND EFFECTS

Doorbell, off
Different doorbell, off
Bang from upstairs

NEW PLAYS

★ **I'LL EAT YOU LAST: A CHAT WITH SUE MENGERS by John Logan.** For more than 20 years, Sue Mengers' clients were the biggest names in show business: Barbra Streisand, Faye Dunaway, Burt Reynolds, Ali MacGraw, Gene Hackman, Cher, Candice Bergen, Ryan O'Neal, Nick Nolte, Mike Nichols, Gore Vidal, Bob Fosse…If her clients were the talk of the town, she was the town, and her dinner parties were the envy of Hollywood. Now, you're invited into her glamorous Beverly Hills home for an evening of dish, dirty secrets and all the inside showbiz details only Sue can tell you. "A delectable soufflé of a solo show…thanks to the buoyant, witty writing of Mr. Logan" –NY Times. "80 irresistible minutes of primo tinseltown dish from a certified master chef." –Hollywood Reporter. [1W] ISBN: 978-0-8222-3079-3

★ **PUNK ROCK by Simon Stephens.** In a private school outside of Manchester, England, a group of highly-articulate seventeen-year-olds flirt and posture their way through the day while preparing for their A-Level mock exams. With hormones raging and minimal adult supervision, the students must prepare for their future — and survive the savagery of high school. Inspired by playwright Simon Stephens' own experiences as a teacher, PUNK ROCK is an honest and unnerving chronicle of contemporary adolescence. "[A] tender, ferocious and frightning play." –NY Times. "[A] muscular little play that starts out funny and ferocious then reveals its compassion by degrees." –Hollywood Reporter. [5M, 3W] ISBN: 978-0-8222-3288-9

★ **THE COUNTRY HOUSE by Donald Margulies.** A brood of famous and longing-to-be-famous creative artists have gathered at their summer home during the Williamstown Theatre Festival. When the weekend takes an unexpected turn, everyone is forced to improvise, inciting a series of simmering jealousies, romantic outbursts, and passionate soul-searching. Both witty and compelling, THE COUNTRY HOUSE provides a piercing look at a family of performers coming to terms with the roles they play in each other's lives. "A valentine to the artists of the stage." –NY Times. "Remarkably candid and funny." –Variety. [3M, 3W] ISBN: 978-0-8222-3274-2

★ **OUR LADY OF KIBEHO by Katori Hall.** Based on real events, OUR LADY OF KIBEHO is an exploration of faith, doubt, and the power and consequences of both. In 1981, a village girl in Rwanda claims to see the Virgin Mary. Ostracized by her schoolmates and labeled disturbed, everyone refuses to believe, until impossible happenings appear again and again. Skepticism gives way to fear, and then to belief, causing upheaval in the school community and beyond. "Transfixing." –NY Times. "Hall's passionate play renews belief in what theater can do." –Time Out [7M, 8W, 1 boy] ISBN: 978-0-8222-3301-5

DRAMATISTS PLAY SERVICE, INC.
440 Park Avenue South, New York, NY 10016 212-683-8960 Fax 212-213-1539
postmaster@dramatists.com www.dramatists.com

NEW PLAYS

★ **AGES OF THE MOON by Sam Shepard.** Byron and Ames are old friends, reunited by mutual desperation. Over bourbon on ice, they sit, reflect and bicker until fifty years of love, friendship and rivalry are put to the test at the barrel of a gun. "A poignant and honest continuation of themes that have always been present in the work of one of this country's most important dramatists, here reconsidered in the light and shadow of time passed." –NY Times. "Finely wrought…as enjoyable and enlightening as a night spent stargazing." –Talkin' Broadway. [2M] ISBN: 978-0-8222-2462-4

★ **ALL THE WAY by Robert Schenkkan. Winner of the 2014 Tony Award for Best Play.** November, 1963. An assassin's bullet catapults Lyndon Baines Johnson into the presidency. A Shakespearean figure of towering ambition and appetite, this charismatic, conflicted Texan hurls himself into the passage of the Civil Rights Act—a tinderbox issue emblematic of a divided America—even as he campaigns for re-election in his own right, and the recognition he so desperately wants. In Pulitzer Prize and Tony Award–winning Robert Schenkkan's vivid dramatization of LBJ's first year in office, means versus ends plays out on the precipice of modern America. ALL THE WAY is a searing, enthralling exploration of the morality of power. It's not personal, it's just politics. "…action-packed, thoroughly gripping… jaw-dropping political drama." –Variety. "A theatrical coup…nonstop action. The suspense of a first-class thriller." –NY1. [17M, 3W] ISBN: 978-0-8222-3181-3

★ **CHOIR BOY by Tarell Alvin McCraney.** The Charles R. Drew Prep School for Boys is dedicated to the creation of strong, ethical black men. Pharus wants nothing more than to take his rightful place as leader of the school's legendary gospel choir. Can he find his way inside the hallowed halls of this institution if he sings in his own key? "[An] affecting and honest portrait…of a gay youth tentatively beginning to find the courage to let the truth about himself become known." –NY Times. "In his stirring and stylishly told drama, Tarell Alvin McCraney cannily explores race and sexuality and the graces and gravity of history." –NY Daily News. [7M] ISBN: 978-0-8222-3116-5

★ **THE ELECTRIC BABY by Stefanie Zadravec.** When Helen causes a car accident that kills a young man, a group of fractured souls cross paths and connect around a mysterious dying baby who glows like the moon. Folk tales and folklore weave throughout this magical story of sad endings, strange beginnings and the unlikely people that get you from one place to the next. "The imperceptible magic that pervades human existence and the power of myth to assuage sorrow are invoked by the playwright as she entwines the lives of strangers in THE ELECTRIC BABY, a touching drama." –NY Times. "As dazzling as the dialogue is dreamful." –Pittsburgh City Paper. [3M, 3W] ISBN: 978-0-8222-3011-3

DRAMATISTS PLAY SERVICE, INC.
440 Park Avenue South, New York, NY 10016 212-683-8960 Fax 212-213-1539
postmaster@dramatists.com www.dramatists.com